The Nuts And Bolts Of Cooperative Learning

David W. Johnson, Roger T. Johnson, and Edythe J. Holubec

Interaction Book Company
7208 Cornelia Drive
Edina, Minnesota 55435
(612) 831-7060

This book is dedicated to the thousands of
teachers who have taken our training in cooperative learning and created classroom environ-
ments where students care about each other
and each other's learning.

ISBN 0-939603-21-7

Table Of Contents

Section Five: Evaluating And Processing

Introduction

The purpose of this book is to provide you with a practical guide to using cooperative learning so you can put cooperative learning to work for you and your students. Read this book carefully and apply its content immediately and often in the classes you teach.

Cooperative learning helps you accomplish a number of important goals simultaneously. **First**, it helps you raise the achievement of all students (gifted, high-achievers, medium achievers, low achievers, academically handicapped). **Second**, it helps you build positive relationships among students that are the heart of creating a learning community in which diversity is valued. **Third**, it gives students the experiences they need for healthy social, psychological, and cognitive development. Cooperative learning's ability to work on these three fronts at the same time separates it from and places it above all other instructional methods. We recommend that in most classrooms, cooperative learning eventually be used 60 to 80 percent of the time. While that may seem extreme to someone who has never used cooperative learning, after finishing reading this book, reaching this goal will seem doable and desirable.

In using cooperative learning you must make a number of preinstructional decisions, explain the learning task and the cooperative procedures to students, monitor the student groups as they work and intervene when necessary, and evaluate the quality of students' learning and help students process how effectively their learning groups are functioning. This constitutes the teacher's role in using cooperative learning. It operationalizes the basic elements (positive interdependence, individual accountability, face-to-face promotive inter-action, social skills, and group processing) that are essential to making learning groups truly cooperative.

This book will be most useful when you read it with one or more colleagues. In reading and discussing this book with colleagues, you are then in position to help each other implement cooperative learning with real fidelity in your classrooms. Implementing cooperative learning, as with all teaching, is like being in love--it always goes better with two.

We would like to thank Laurie Stevahn and Linda Johnson for their help in editing and preparing the graphics for this book. Their creativity and hard work are deeply appreciated. We wish to thank Thomas Grummett for most of the drawings in this book.

Section One: Understanding Cooperative Learning

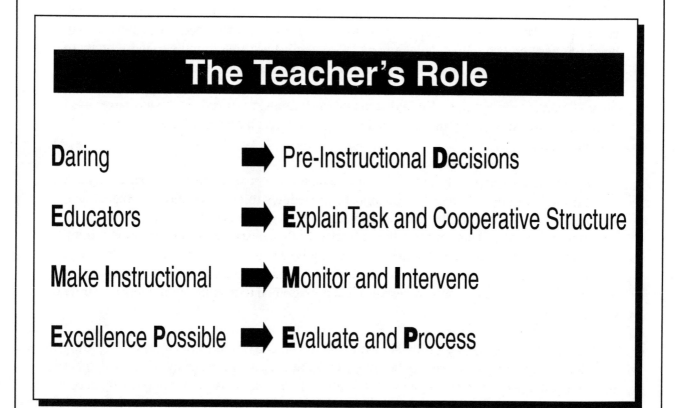

Chapter One: Cooperative Learning

Introduction

At age 55, after his defeat by Woodrow Wilson for President of the United States, Teddy Roosevelt took a journey to South America. The Brazilian Government suggested he lead an expedition to explore a vast, unmapped river deep in the jungle. Known as the River of Doubt, it was believed to be a tributary to the Amazon. Roosevelt accepted instantly. *"We will go down the unknown river,"* he declared, and the Brazilian government organized an expedition for the trip. *"I had to go,"* he said later, *"it was my last chance to be a boy."* Roosevelt, with his son Kermit and a party of eighteen, headed into the jungle. *"On February 27, 1914, shortly after midday, we started down the River of Doubt into the unknown,"* Roosevelt wrote. The jouney was an ordeal. Hostile Indians harrassed them. Five canoes were shattered and had to be rebuilt. Their food ran short and valuable equipment was lost. One man drowned when his canoe capsized. Another went berserk and killed a member of the expedition and then disappeared into the wilderness. Roosevelt, ill with fever, badly injured his leg when he tried to keep two capsized canoes from being smashed against rocks. Unable to walk, he had to be carried. Lying in a tent with an infected leg and a temperature of 105, he requested to be left behind. Ignoring such pleas, Kermit brought his father to safety with the help of the other members of the expedition. Teddy Roosevelt barely survived, but he and his companions accomplished their mission. The party mapped the 1000 mile River of Doubt and collected priceless specimens for the Museum of Natural History. The river was renamed in his honor, **Rio Theodore**.

An expedition such as Roosevelt's consists of four phases:

1. You make a series of pre-journey decisions about the number of people needed, the materials and equipment required, and the route to be taken.

2. You brief all participants on the goals and objectives of the journey, emphasize that members' survival depends on the joint efforts of all, and the behaviors you expect of members of the expedition.

Teacher's Role

3. You make the journey, carefully mapping the area traveled and collecting the targeted specimens.

4. You report your findings to interested parties, reflect on what went right and wrong with fellow members, and write your memoirs.

Conducting a cooperative lesson is done in the same way. You, the teacher, make a number of preinstructional decisions, explain to students the instructional task and the cooperative nature of the lesson, conduct the lesson, and evaluate and process the results. More specifically, you:

1. **Make Preinstructional Decisions:** In every lesson you (a) formulate objectives, (b) decide on the size of groups, (c) choose a method for assigning students to groups, (d) decide which roles to assign group members, (e) arrange the room, and (f) arrange the materials students need to complete the assignment.

2. **Explain the Task and Cooperative Structure:** In every lesson you (a) explain the academic assignment to students, (b) explain the criteria for success, (c) structure positive interdependence, (d) explain the individual accountability, and (e) explain the behaviors you expect to see during the lesson.

3. **Monitor and Intervene:** While you (a) conduct the lesson, you (b) monitor each learning group and (c) intervene when needed to improve taskwork and teamwork, and (d) bring closure to the lesson.

4. **Evaluate and Process:** You (a) assess and evaluate the quality and quantity of student achievement, (b) ensure students carefully process the effectiveness of their learning groups, (c) have students make a plan for improvement, and (d) have students celebrate the hard work of group members.

The purpose of this book is to provide detailed and specific practical guidance for conducting cooperative lessons. Each chapter explains an important step in structuring cooperative learning and gives detailed practice help for implementing it. In order to take full advantage of the practical guidance given, however, you need to know what cooperative learning is and why it is important to use it.

What Is Cooperative Learning?

Cooperation is working together to accomplish shared goals. Within cooperative situations, individuals seek outcomes that are beneficial to themselves and beneficial to all other group members. **Cooperative learning** is the instructional use of small groups so that students work together to maximize their own and each other's learning. It may be contrasted with **competitive** (students work against each other to achieve an academic goal such as a grade of "A" that only one or a few students can attain) and **individualistic** (students work by themselves to accomplish learning goals unrelated to those of the other students) learning. In cooperative and individualistic learning, you evaluate student efforts on a criteria-referenced basis while in competitive learning you grade students on a norm-referenced basis. While there are limitations on when and where you may use competitive and individualistic learning appropriately, you may structure any learning task in any subject area with any curriculum cooperatively.

Why Use Cooperative Learning?

The conviction to use cooperative learning flows from knowing the research. Since the first research study was published in 1898, there have been nearly 600 experimental and over 100 correlational studies conducted on cooperative, competitive, and individualistic efforts (see Johnson & Johnson, 1989 for a complete review of these studies). The multiple outcomes studied can be classified into three major categories (see Figure 1.3): efforts to achieve, positive relationships, and psychological health. From the research, we know that cooperation, compared with competitive and individualistic efforts, typically results in:

1. **Greater Efforts To Achieve:** This includes higher achievement and greater productivity by all students (high-, medium-, and low-achievers), long-term retention, intrinsic motivation, achievement motivation, time-on-task, higher-level reasoning, and critical thinking.

2. **More Positive Relationships Among Students:** This includes esprit-de-

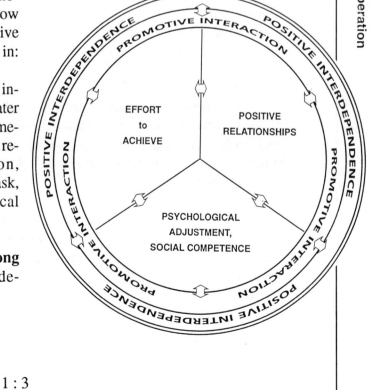

1 : 3

corps, caring and committed relationships, personal and academic social support, valuing of diversity, and cohesion.

3. **Greater Psychological Health:** This includes general psychological adjustment, ego-strength, social development, social competencies, self-esteem, self-identity, and ability to cope with adversity and stress.

The powerful effects of cooperation on so many important outcomes separates it from other instructional methods and makes it one of your most important instructional tools.

Types Of Cooperative Learning Groups

There are three types of cooperative learning groups. **Formal cooperative learning** groups last from one class period to several weeks. You may structure any academic assignment or course requirement for formal cooperative learning. Formal cooperative learning groups ensure that students are actively involved in the intellectual work of organizing material, explaining it, summarizing it, and integrating it into existing conceptual structures. They are the heart of using cooperative learning. **Informal cooperative learning** groups are ad-hoc groups that last from a few minutes to one class period. You use them during direct teaching (lectures, demonstrations, films, videos) to focus student attention on the material they are to learn, set a mood conducive to learning, help set expectations as to what the lesson will cover, ensure that students cognitively process the material you are teaching, and provide closure to an instructional session. **Cooperative base groups** are long-term (lasting for at least a year), heterogeneous groups with stable membership whose primary purpose is for members to give each other the support, help, encouragement, and assistance each needs to progress academically. Base groups provide students with long-term, committed relationships.

In addition to the three types of cooperative learning, **cooperative learning scripts** are standard cooperative procedures for (a) conducting generic, repetitive lessons (such as writing reports or giving presentations) and (b) managing classroom routines (such as checking homework and reviewing a test). Once planned and conducted several times, scripted repetitive cooperative lessons and classroom routines become automatic activities in the classroom.

When you use formal, informal, and cooperative base groups repeatedly, you will gain a routine-level of expertise in doing so. **Expertise** is reflected in your proficiency, adroitness, competence, and skill in doing something. Expertise in structuring cooperative efforts is reflected in your being able to:

TYPES OF COOPERATIVE LEARNING

FORMAL	INFORMAL	BASE GROUPS
_____	_____	_____
_____	_____	_____
_____	_____	_____
_____	_____	_____
_____	_____	_____
_____	_____	_____
_____	_____	_____

1. Take any lesson in any subject area with any age student and structure it cooperatively.

2. Use cooperative learning (at a routine-use level) 60 to 80 percent of the time.

3. Describe precisely what you are doing and why in order to (a) communicate to others the nature and advantages of cooperative learning and (b) teach colleagues how to implement cooperative learning.

4. Apply the principles of cooperation to other settings, such as colleagial relationships and faculty meetings.

You usually gain such expertise through a progressive-refinement procedure of (a) teaching a cooperative lesson, (b) assessing how well it went, (c) reflecting on how cooperation could have been better structured, and then (d) teaching an improved cooperative lesson, (b) assessing how well it went, and so forth. You thus gain experience in an incremental step-by-step manner. The **routine-use level of teacher expertise** is the ability to structure cooperative learning situations automatically without conscious thought or planning. You can then use cooperative learning with fidelity for the rest of your teaching career.

What Kind Of Group Am I Using?

There is nothing magical about working in a group. Some kinds of learning groups facilitate student learning and increase the quality of life in the classroom. Other types of learning groups hinder student learning and create disharmony and dissatisfaction with classroom life. To use cooperative learning effectively, you must know what is and is not a cooperative group.

There are many kinds of groups that can be used in the classroom. Cooperative learning groups are just one of them. When you use instructional groups, you have to ask yourself, "*What type of group am I using?*" The following checklist may be helpful in answering that question.

1. **Pseudo-Learning Group:** Students are assigned to work together but they have no interest in doing so. They believe they will be evaluated by being ranked from the highest performer to the lowest performer. While on the surface students talk to each other, under the surface they are competing. They see each other as rivals who must be defeated, block or interfere with each other's learning, hide information from each other, attempt to mislead and confuse each other, and distrust each other. The result is that the sum of the whole is less than the potential of the individual members. Students would achieve more if they were working alone.

2. **Traditional Classroom Learning Group:** Students are assigned to work together and accept that they have to do so. Assignments are structured, however, so that very little joint work is required. Students believe that they will be evaluated and rewarded as individuals, not as members of the group. They interact primarily to clarify how assignments are to be done. They seek each other's information, but have no motivation to teach what they know to their groupmates. Helping and sharing is minimized. Some students loaf, seeking a free ride on the efforts of their more conscientious groupmates. The conscientious members feel exploited and do less. The result is that the sum of the whole is more than the potential of some of the members, but the more hard working and conscientious students would perform higher if they worked alone.

3. **Cooperative Learning Group:** Students are assigned to work together and they are happy to do so. They believe that their success depends on the efforts of all group members. There are five defining characteristics. **First,** the group goal of maximizing all members' learning provides a compelling common purpose that motivates members to roll up their sleeves and accomplish something beyond their individual achievements. Members believe that "they sink or swim together," and "if one of us fails, we all fail." **Second**, group members

hold themselves and each other accountable for doing high quality work to achieve their mutual goals. **Third,** group members work face-to-face to produce joint work-products. They do real work together. Students promote each other's success through helping, sharing, assisting, explaining, and encouraging. They provide both academic and personal support based on a commitment to and caring about each other. **Fourth,** group members are taught social skills and are expected to use them to coordinate their efforts and achieve their goals. Both taskwork and teamwork skills are emphasized. All members accept the responsibility for providing leadership. **Finally,** groups

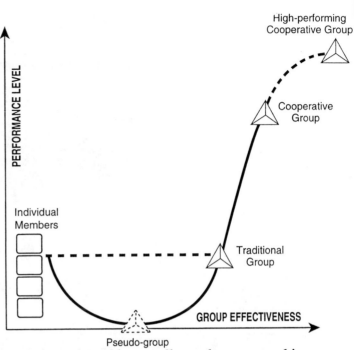

Figure 4.2 The Group Performance Curve

analyze how effectively they are achieving their goals and how well members are working together. There is an emphasis on continuous improvement of the quality of learning and teamwork processes. The result is that the group is more than a sum of its parts and all students perform higher academically than they would if they worked alone.

4. **High-Performance Cooperative Learning Group:** This is a group that meets all the criteria for being a cooperative learning group and outperforms all reasonable expectations, given its membership. What differentiates the high-performance group from the cooperative learning group is the level of commitment members have to each other and the group's success. Jennifer Futernick, who is part of a high-performing, rapid response team at McKinsey & Company, calls the emotion binding her teammates together a form of love (Katzenbach & Smith, 1993). Ken Hoepner of the Burlington Northern Intermodal Team (also described by Katzenbach and Smith, 1993) stated: "*Not only did we trust each other, not only did we respect each other, but we gave a damn about the rest of the people on this team. If we saw somebody vulnerable, we were there to help.*" Members' mutual concern for each other's personal growth enables high-performance cooperative groups to perform far above expectations, and also to have lots of fun. The bad news about high-performance cooperative groups is that they are rare. Most groups never achieve this level of development.

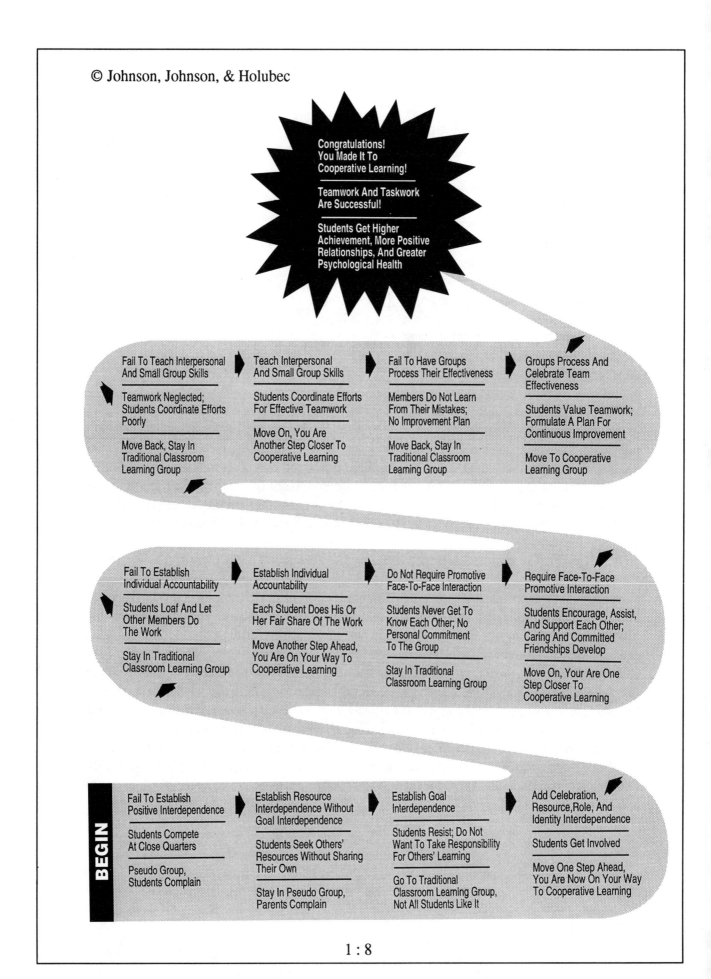

© Johnson, Johnson, & Holubec

Congratulations! You Made It To Cooperative Learning!

Teamwork And Taskwork Are Successful!

Students Get Higher Achievement, More Positive Relationships, And Greater Psychological Health

Fail To Teach Interpersonal And Small Group Skills

Teamwork Neglected; Students Coordinate Efforts Poorly

Move Back, Stay In Traditional Classroom Learning Group

Teach Interpersonal And Small Group Skills

Students Coordinate Efforts For Effective Teamwork

Move On, You Are Another Step Closer To Cooperative Learning

Fail To Have Groups Process Their Effectiveness

Members Do Not Learn From Their Mistakes; No Improvement Plan

Move Back, Stay In Traditional Classroom Learning Group

Groups Process And Celebrate Team Effectiveness

Students Value Teamwork; Formulate A Plan For Continuous Improvement

Move To Cooperative Learning Group

Fail To Establish Individual Accountability

Students Loaf And Let Other Members Do The Work

Stay In Traditional Classroom Learning Group

Establish Individual Accountability

Each Student Does His Or Her Fair Share Of The Work

Move Another Step Ahead, You Are On Your Way To Cooperative Learning

Do Not Require Promotive Face-To-Face Interaction

Students Never Get To Know Each Other; No Personal Commitment To The Group

Stay In Traditional Classroom Learning Group

Require Face-To-Face Promotive Interaction

Students Encourage, Assist, And Support Each Other; Caring And Committed Friendships Develop

Move On, Your Are One Step Closer To Cooperative Learning

BEGIN

Fail To Establish Positive Interdependence

Students Compete At Close Quarters

Pseudo Group, Students Complain

Establish Resource Interdependence Without Goal Interdependence

Students Seek Others' Resources Without Sharing Their Own

Stay In Pseudo Group, Parents Complain

Establish Goal Interdependence

Students Resist; Do Not Want To Take Responsibility For Others' Learning

Go To Traditional Classroom Learning Group, Not All Students Like It

Add Celebration, Resource,Role, And Identity Interdependence

Students Get Involved

Move One Step Ahead, You Are Now On Your Way To Cooperative Learning

1 : 8

To use cooperative learning effectively, you must realize that not all groups are cooperative groups. The learning group performance curve illustrates that how well any small group performs depends on how it is structured (Figure 1.1) (Katzenbach & Smith, 1993). Placing people in the same room and calling them a cooperative group does not make them one. Study groups, project groups, lab groups, home rooms, reading groups are groups, but they are not necessarily cooperative. Even with the best of intentions, you may find traditional classroom learning groups on your hands rather than cooperative learning groups. Your job is to form students into learning groups, diagnose where on the group performance curve the groups are, keep strengthening the basic elements of cooperation, and move the groups up the performance curve until they are truly cooperative learning groups.

What Makes Cooperation Work

Together we stand, divided we fall.

Watchword Of The American Revolution

To structure lessons so students do in fact work cooperatively with each other, you must understand the basic elements that make cooperation work. Mastering the basic elements of cooperation allows you to:

1. Take your existing lessons, curricula, and courses and structure them cooperatively.

2. Tailor cooperative learning lessons to your unique instructional needs, circumstances, curricula, subject areas, and students.

3. Diagnose the problems some students may have in working together and intervene to increase the effectiveness of the student learning groups.

For cooperation to work well, you explicitly have to structure five essential elements in each lesson (see Figure 1.2). **The first and most important element is positive interdependence.** You must give a clear task and a group goal so that students believe they "*sink or swim together.*" You have successfully structured positive interdependence when group members perceive that they are linked with each other in a way that one cannot succeed unless everyone succeeds. If one fails, all fail. Group members realize, therefore, that each person's efforts benefit not only him- or herself, but all other group members as well. Positive interdependence creates a commitment to other people's success as well as one's own and is the heart of cooperative learning. If there is no positive interdependence, there is no cooperation.

The second essential element of cooperative learning is individual and group accountability. The group must be accountable for achieving its goals. Each member must be accountable for contributing his or her share of the work (which ensures that no one can "hitch-hike" on the work of others). The group has to be clear about its goals and be able to measure (a) its progress in achieving them and (b) the individual efforts of each of its members. **Individual accountability** exists when the performance of each individual student is assessed and the results are given back to the group and the individual in order to ascertain who needs more assistance, support, and encouragement in completing the assignment. The purpose of cooperative learning groups is to make each member a stronger individual in his or her right. Students learn together so that they can subsequently perform higher as individuals.

The third essential component of cooperative learning is promotive interaction, preferably face-to-face. Students need to do real work together in which they promote each other's success by sharing resources and helping, supporting, encouraging, and praising each other's efforts to learn. Cooperative learning groups are both an academic support system (every student has someone who is committed to helping him or her learn) and a personal support system (every student has someone who is committed to him or her as a person). There are important cognitive activities and interpersonal dynamics that can only occur when students promote each other's learning. This includes orally explaining how to solve problems, discussing the nature of the concepts being learned, teaching one's knowledge to classmates, and connecting present with past learning. It is through promoting each other's learning face-to-face that members become personally committed to each other as well as to their mutual goals.

The fourth essential element of cooperative learning is teaching students the required interpersonal and small group skills. In cooperative learning groups students are required to learn academic subject matter (taskwork) and also to learn the interpersonal and small group skills required to function as part of a group (teamwork). Cooperative learning is inherently more complex than competitive or individualistic learning because students have to engage simultaneously in taskwork and teamwork. Group members must know how to provide effective leadership, decision-making, trust-building, communication, and conflict-management, and be motivated to use the prerequisite skills. You have to teach teamwork skills just as purposefully and precisely as you do academic skills. Since cooperation and conflict are inherently related (see Johnson & Johnson, 1991, 1992), the procedures and skills for managing conflicts constructively are especially important for the long-term success of learning groups. Procedures and strategies for teaching students social skills may be found in Johnson (1991, 1993) and Johnson and F. Johnson (1994).

The fifth essential component of cooperative learning is group processing. Group processing exists when group members discuss how well they are achieving their goals and maintaining effective working relationships. Groups need to describe what member actions are helpful and unhelpful and make decisions about what behaviors to continue or change. Continuous improvement of the process of learning results from the careful analysis of how members are working together and determining how group effectiveness can be enhanced.

Your use of cooperative learning becomes effective through disciplined action. The five basic elements are not just characteristics of good cooperative learning groups. They are a discipline that you have to rigorously apply(much like a diet has to be adhered to) to produce the conditions for effective cooperative action.

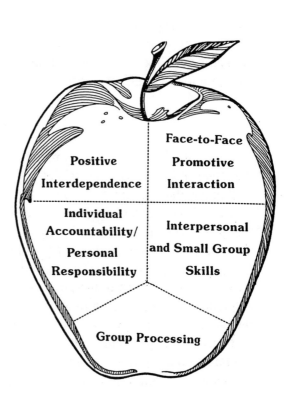

The Underlying Organizational Structure

W. Edwards Deming, J. Juran, and other founders of the quality movement have stated that more than 85 percent of the behavior of members of an organization is directly attributable to the organization's structure, not the nature of the individuals involved. Your classroom is no exception. If competitive or individualistic learning dominates your classroom, your students will behave accordingly, regardless of whether you have temporarily put them in cooperative groups. If cooperative learning dominates your classroom, your students will behave accordingly and a true learning community will result.

The issue of cooperation among students is part of a larger issue of the organizational structure of schools (Johnson & Johnson, 1994). For decades schools have functioned as "*mass production*" organizations that divided work into component parts (first grade, second grade; English, social studies, science) to be performed by teachers who are isolated from their colleagues and work alone, in their own room, with their own set of students, and with their own set of curriculum materials. Students can be assigned to any teacher because students are considered to be interchangeable parts in the education machine. By using cooperative learning the majority of the time you are changing the basic organizational structure of your classroom to a team-based, high-performance one. In other words, cooperation is more than an instructional procedure. It is a basic shift in organizational structure that will affect all aspects of classroom life.

Summary

Great missions are not accomplished alone. Teddy Roosevelt could not have explored the River of Doubt by himself. It took the cooperative efforts of twenty people to meet the challenges that journey presented. Journeys of learning are similar. While lessons can be structured so that students compete, work individualistically, or cooperate, it is cooperation that most powerfully affects instructional outcomes. There are three types of cooperative learning groups--formal, informal, and base groups. Not all groups, however, are cooperative groups. Teachers may use pseudo groups or traditional learning groups. In order to ensure that groups are cooperative groups, teachers have to be able to implement five basic elements into every lesson (positive interdependence, individual accountability, promotive interaction, social skills, group processing). Cooperative learning, furthermore, is more than an instructional procedure. It sets the stage for creating a team-based, high-performance organizational structure in the classroom and the school. Gaining expertise in using cooperative learning, however, is not easy. It takes years of training and practice to refine one's competencies in using cooperative learning effectively.

Making a journey requires planning, briefing of all members, traveling, and reflecting on the experience. Cooperative learning goes through the same phases. The teacher's role in using cooperative learning consists of four parts. Teachers have to plan the lesson, making a number of preinstructional decisions. Then they have to explain the academic task and the nature of the joint effort to students. Teachers conduct the lesson while monitoring the learning groups and intervening when it is necessary. Finally, teachers evaluate the quality of students' academic work and ensure students process how effectively they are working together in their learning groups. Each of these phases will be explained in this book, beginning with the preinstructional decisions required to plan an effective cooperative lesson.

The Teacher's Role in Cooperation Learning

Make Pre-Instructional Decisions

Specify Academic and Social Skills Objectives. Every lesson has both (a) academic and (b) interpersonal and small group skills objectives.

Decide on Group Size. Learning groups should be small (groups of two or three students, four at the most).

Decide on Group Composition (Assign Students to Groups). Assign students to groups randomly or select groups yourself. Usually you will wish to maximize the heterogeneity in each group.

Assign Roles. Structure student-student interaction by assigning roles such as Reader, Recorder, Encourager of Participation, and Checker for Understanding.

Arrange the Room. Group members should be "knee to knee and eye to eye" but arranged so they all can see you at the front of the room.

Plan Materials. Arrange materials to give a "sink or swim together" message. Give only one paper to the group or give each member part of the material to be learned.

Explain Task And Cooperative Structure

Explain the Academic Task. Explain the task, the objectives of the lesson, the concepts and principles students need to know to complete the assignment, and the procedures they are to follow.

Explain the Criteria for Success. Student work should be evaluated on a criteria-referenced basis. Make clear your criteria for evaluating students' work.

Structure Positive Interdependence. Students must believe that they "sink or swim together." Always establish mutual goals (students are responsible for own learning and the learning of all other group members). Supplement goal interdependence with celebration/reward, resource, role, and identity interdependence.

Structure Intergroup Cooperation. Have groups check with and help other groups. Extend the benefits of cooperation to the whole class.

Structure Individual Accountability. Each student must feel responsible for doing his or her fair share of the work. Ways to ensure accountability are frequent oral quizzing of group members picked at random, individual tests, and assigning a member the role of Checker for Understanding.

Specify Expected Behaviors. The more specific you are about the behaviors you want to see in the groups, the more likely students will do them. Social skills may be classified as **forming** (staying with the group, using quiet voices), **functioning** (contributing, encouraging others to participate), **formulating** (summarizing, elaborating), and **fermenting** (criticizing ideas, asking for justification). Regularly teach the interpersonal and small group skills you wish to see used in the learning groups.

Monitor And Intervene

Arrange Face-to-Face Promotive Interaction. Conduct the lesson in ways that ensure that students promote each other's success face-to-face.

Monitor Students' Behavior. This is the fun part! While students are working, you circulate to see whether they understand the assignment and the material, give immediate feedback and reinforcement, and praise good use of group skills. Collect observation data on each group and student.

Intervene to Improve Taskwork and Teamwork. Provide **task assistance** (clarify, reteach) if students do not understand the assignment. Provide **teamwork assistance** if students are having difficulties in working together productively.

Provide Closure. To enhance student learning have students summarize the major points in the lesson or review important facts.

Evaluate And Process

Evaluate Student Learning. Assess and evaluate the quality and quantity of student learning. Involve students in the assessment process.

Process Group Functioning. Ensure each student receives feedback, analyzes the data on group functioning, sets an improvement goal, and participates in a team celebration. Have groups routinely list three things they did well in working together and one thing they will do better tomorrow. Summarize as a whole class. Have groups celebrate their success and hard work.

Cooperative Lesson Planning Form

Grade Level: _____ Subject Area: _____ Date:_____

Lesson: _____

Objectives:

1. Academic
2. Social

Decisions:

1. Group Size: _____
2. Method Of Assigning Students: _____
3. Roles: _____

   _____

4. Room Arrangement: _____
5. Materials _____

   ❏   a.   One Copy Per Group

   ❏   b.   Jigsaw

   ❏   c.   Tournament

   ❏   d.   One Copy Per Person

   ❏   e.   Other

Explaining Task And Goal Structure

1. Task:_____

   _____

2. Criteria For Success: _____

   _____

3. Positive Interdependence: _____

   _____

4. Individual Accountability: _____

   _____

5. Intergroup Cooperation: _____

   _____

6. Expected Behaviors: _____

   _____

Monitoring And Intervening

1. Observation Procedure: _____ Formal _____ Informal

2. Observations By: _____ Teacher _____ Students _____ Visitors

3. Intervening For Task Assistance: _____
   _____

4. Intervening For Teamwork Assistance: _____
   _____

4. Other: _____
   _____

Evaluating and Processing

1. Assessment Of Members' Individual Learning: _____
   _____

2. Assessment Of Group Productivity: _____
   _____

3. Small Group Processing: _____
   _____

4. Whole Class Processing: _____
   _____

5. Charts And Graphs Used: _____
   _____

6. Positive Feedback To Each Student: _____
   _____

7. Goal Setting For Improvement: _____
   _____

8. Celebration: _____
   _____

9. Other: _____

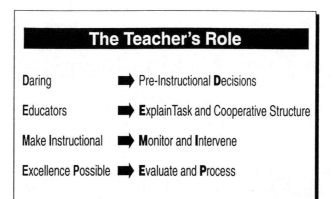

The Teacher's Role

Daring	➡	Pre-Instructional **D**ecisions
Educators	➡	**Ex**plainTask and Cooperative Structure
Make Instructional	➡	**M**onitor and **I**ntervene
Excellence Possible	➡	**E**valuate and **P**rocess

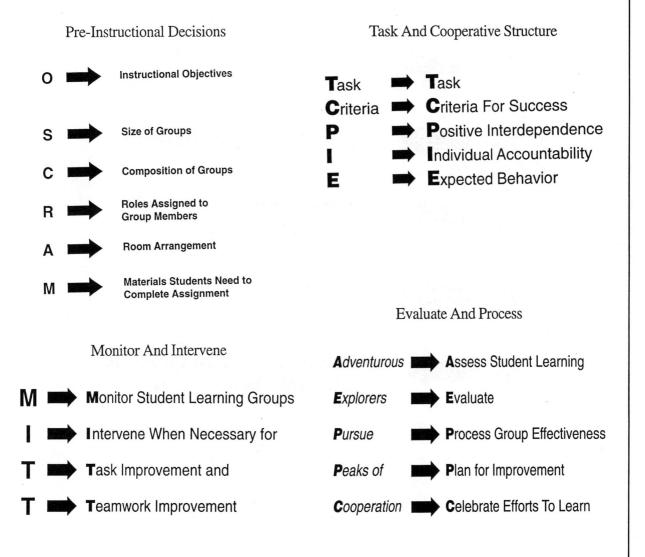

Pre-Instructional Decisions

O ➡ **Instructional Objectives**

S ➡ **Size of Groups**

C ➡ **Composition of Groups**

R ➡ **Roles Assigned to Group Members**

A ➡ **Room Arrangement**

M ➡ **Materials Students Need to Complete Assignment**

Task And Cooperative Structure

Task ➡ **T**ask

Criteria ➡ **C**riteria For Success

P ➡ **P**ositive Interdependence

I ➡ **I**ndividual Accountability

E ➡ **E**xpected Behavior

Monitor And Intervene

M ➡ **M**onitor Student Learning Groups

I ➡ **I**ntervene When Necessary for

T ➡ **T**ask Improvement and

T ➡ **T**eamwork Improvement

Evaluate And Process

Adventurous ➡ **A**ssess Student Learning

Explorers ➡ **E**valuate

Pursue ➡ **P**rocess Group Effectiveness

Peaks of ➡ **P**lan for Improvement

Cooperation ➡ **C**elebrate Efforts To Learn

Section Two: Making Preinstructional Decisions

O  **Instructional Objectives**

S  **Size of Groups**

C  **Composition of Groups**

R  **Roles Assigned to Group Members**

A **Room Arrangement**

M **Materials Students Need to Complete Assignment**

Chapter Two: Specifying Objectives

The Roman philosopher Seneca once said, *"When you do not know to which port you are sailing, no wind is favorable."* The same may be said for teaching. There is no way to plan for a lesson unless you know what the lesson is aimed at accomplishing. You need instructional objectives. There are two types of objectives that a teacher needs to specify before the lesson begins. You need to specify the **academic objective** at the correct level for the students and matched to the right level of instruction according to a conceptual or task analysis. The **social skills objective** details what interpersonal and small group skills you wish to emphasize during the lesson.

Every lesson has both academic objectives that define what students are to learn and social skills objectives needed to train students to cooperate effectively with each other. In planning the objectives for the lesson, you, the teacher, decide which interpersonal and small group skills to emphasize. There are a number of ways you may choose a social skill.

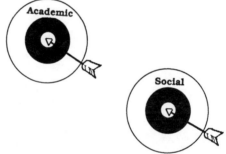

1. You ask students which social skills would improve their teamwork and choose one of the skills suggested.

2. You keep a list of social skills that you teach to every class. The next one on the list becomes the skill emphasized in today's lesson. Some lessons require specific social skills as part of completing the assignment. In such cases, the nature of the lesson dictates which social skills you emphasize.

3. You monitor the learning groups and diagnose specific problems the students are having in working with each other. You then teach a social skill students can use to solve the problem.

You draw a picture (flow chart) of how the group actually completes the assignment and maximizes the learning of each member. The process required to complete the lesson may suggest or even require certain social skills. A **Flow Chart** is a simple yet powerful visual tool to display all the steps in a process. You create a flow chart by:

1. Clearly defining where the learning process begins and ends and what are the inputs and the outputs. This is known as defining the boundaries.

2. Identifying all the steps the process actually follows (the key steps, who is involved, and who does what, when).

3. Drawing the steps in sequence.

4. Observing what the group actually does.

5. Comparing actual performance with the flow chart. Either revise the flow chart or plan how to increase the quality with which group members engage in each step.

Students may continually revise the flow chart as they refine and streamline their efforts. As the process of learning gets refined, the need for certain new social skills may become apparent.

Flow Chart: Academic And Social Skills Required To Pair Read A Passage And Answer Comprehension Questions

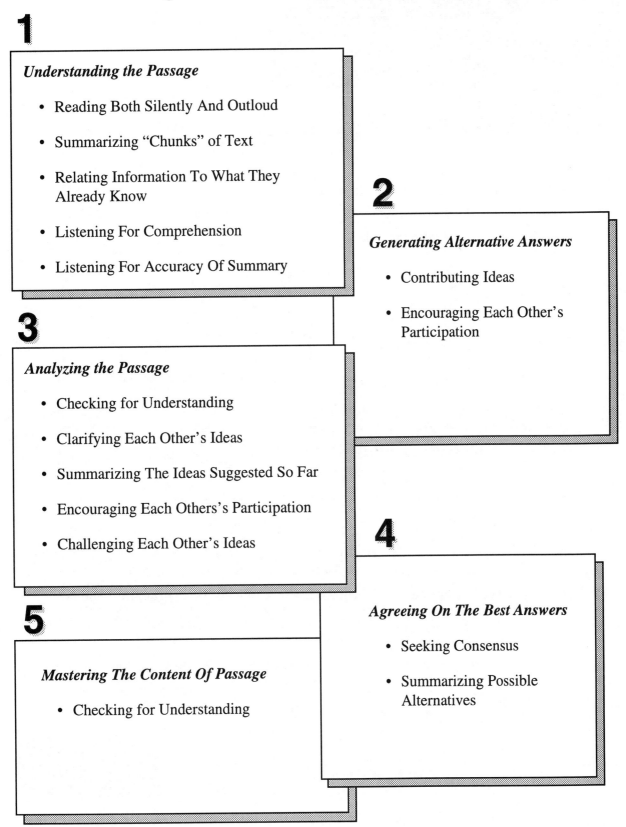

1

Understanding the Passage

- Reading Both Silently And Outloud
- Summarizing "Chunks" of Text
- Relating Information To What They Already Know
- Listening For Comprehension
- Listening For Accuracy Of Summary

2

Generating Alternative Answers

- Contributing Ideas
- Encouraging Each Other's Participation

3

Analyzing the Passage

- Checking for Understanding
- Clarifying Each Other's Ideas
- Summarizing The Ideas Suggested So Far
- Encouraging Each Others's Participation
- Challenging Each Other's Ideas

4

Agreeing On The Best Answers

- Seeking Consensus
- Summarizing Possible Alternatives

5

Mastering The Content Of Passage

- Checking for Understanding

Data Processing

The purpose of the several warm-ups on this page is that of Getting to Know You! None include the use of silicon chips, but are guaranteed to provide a leg up on introductions.

Have students arrange themselves in a line by height. *Mingle -- with those shorter types heading for the front of the line, taller in back. Let's see how quickly we can get things sorted out. Oh . . . one little twist: I'd like you to keep your eyes closed for this process!* Now if you really want to make things difficult, also tell them they cannot talk!

• • • • •

Another line-up might use first names, in alphabetical order. This might prove just a bit faster than the preceding method!

• • • • •

Or groups can be sorted out by states . . . where was each person born? Maybe even favorite ice cream flavors. Come up with a variety of data bits that can be used for the same purpose.

• • • • •

And another variation on Birthdays: Sort out a line in chronological order of birth. With a group of 25, there's a better than 50/50 chance that you'll have two standing side -- with the same birthday! When students are all lined up by birthdays, they can reel them off in order, from New Year's Day to New Year's Eve. (You might even encourage group cheers for each of the Zodiac signs!)

© Johnson, Johnson, & Holubec

Chapter Three: Assigning Students To Groups

There is a folk saying about snowflakes. Each one is so fragile and small. But when they stick together, it is amazing what they can do. The same is true for people. When we work together, there is no limit to human ingenuity and potential. For students to work together, they must be assigned to groups. To assign students to groups, you must decide how large a group should be, how students should be assigned to a group, how long the groups will exist, and what combination of groups will be used in the lesson.

Who Works With Whom

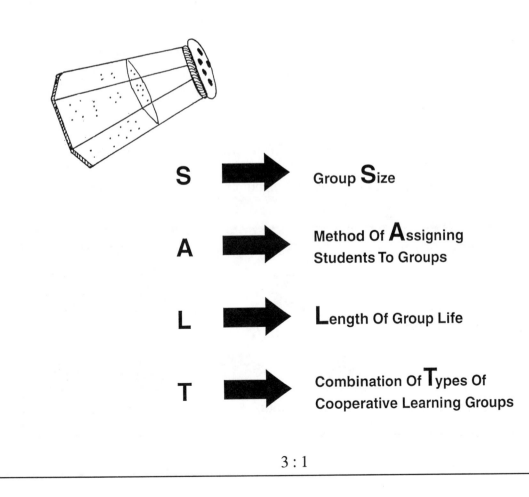

S ➡ Group **S**ize

A ➡ Method Of **A**ssigning Students To Groups

L ➡ **L**ength Of Group Life

T ➡ Combination Of **T**ypes Of Cooperative Learning Groups

Deciding on the Size of the Group

Sic parvis magna (Great things have small beginnings).

Sir Francis Drake's Motto

There is no ideal size for a cooperative learning group. The size of a cooperative learning group depends on the objectives of the lesson, students' age and experience in working in teams, the curriculum materials and equipment available, and the time limits imposed on the lesson. While cooperative learning groups typically range in size from two to four, **the basic rule of thumb is, "The smaller the better."** When in doubt, assign students to pairs or triads. In selecting the size of a cooperative learning group, however, there are a number of factors to take into account. You need to remember:

1. **As the size of the learning group increases, the range of abilities, expertise, skills, and the number of minds available for acquiring and processing information increase.** As the size of the group increases, so does the richness of diversity of viewpoints. With the addition of each group member, the resources to help the group succeed increase.

2. **The shorter the period of time available, the smaller the learning group should be.** If there is only a brief period of time available for the lesson, then smaller groups such as pairs will be more effective because they take less time to get organized, they operate faster, and there is more "air time" per member.

3. **The smaller the group, the more difficult it is for students to hide and not contribute their share of the work.** Small groups increase the visibility of students' efforts and thereby make them more accountable.

4. **The larger the group, the more skillful group members must be** in such things as providing everyone with a chance to speak, coordinating the actions of group members, reaching consensus, ensuring explanation and elaboration of the material being learned,

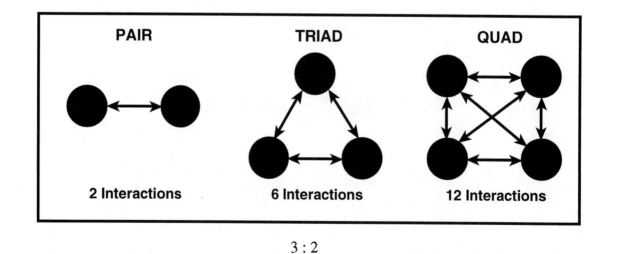

keeping all members on task, and maintaining good working relationships. Within a pair, students have to manage two interactions. Within a group of three, there are six interactions to manage. Within a group of four, there are twelve interactions to manage. As the size of the group increases, the interpersonal and small group skills required to manage the interactions among group members become far more complex and sophisticated. Very few students have the social skills needed for effective group functioning even for small groups. A common mistake made by many teachers is to have students work in groups of four, five, and six members before the students have the skills to do so competently.

5. **With increasing group size, there is a decrease in face-to-face interaction among teammates and a reduced sense of intimacy.** What results is less group cohesion, fewer friendships, and less personal support among members.

6. **The materials available or the specific nature of the task may dictate a group size.** When you have ten computers and thirty students, you may wish to assign students to groups of three. When the task is practice tennis, group size of two seems natural.

7. **The smaller the group, the easier it is to identify any difficulties students have in working together.** Problems in leadership, unresolved conflicts among group members, issues over power and control, and other problems students have in working together are more visible and apparent when groups are small.

The involvement of members is partially determined by the size of the group. When groups get too large, it is easy for students to sit back and wait for others to do the work. One of the reasons for using cooperative learning is to ensure that you actively engage students in learning. Groups need to be small enough to ensure the active involvement of all students. When you monitor cooperative learning groups, you may wish to see if all members participate equally. If not, you may wish to decrease the size of the groups.

Assigning Students to Groups

There is no ideal group membership. What determines a group's productivity is not who its members are, but rather members' teamwork skills. Training students in how to work together effectively will have far greater effect on group productivity than will the specific students assigned to a group. There are, however, a number of methods you may use to assign students to groups.

Before you assign students to groups, you must decide whether the learning groups should be homogeneous or heterogeneous? There are times when you may use cooperative learning

The Group Size Wheel

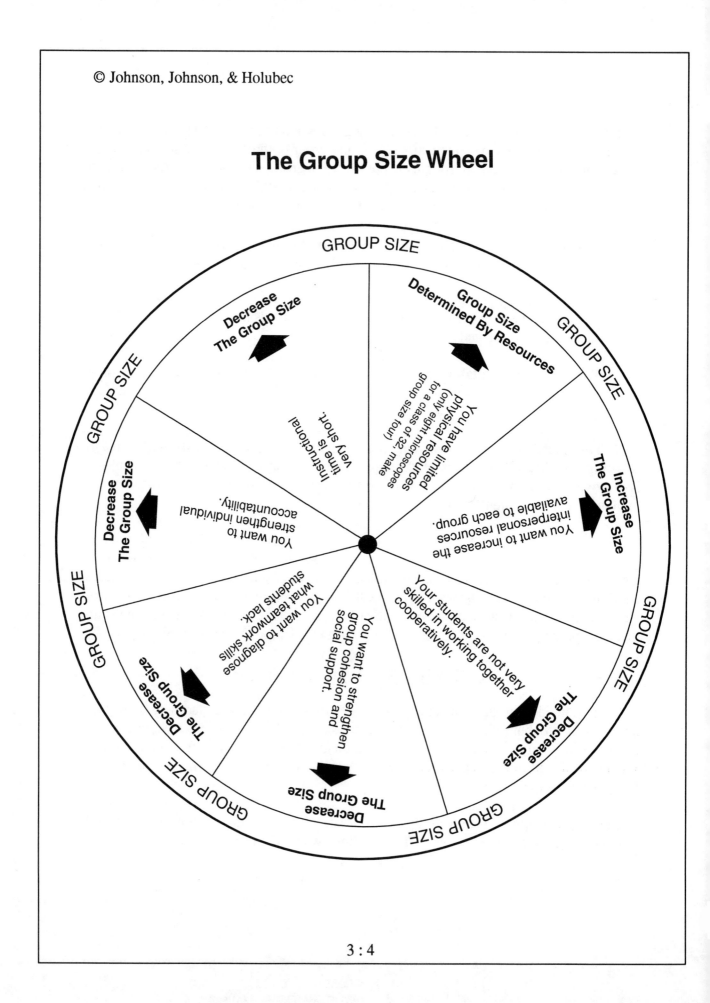

groups that are homogeneous in ability to teach specific skills or to achieve certain instructional objectives. Generally, however, there are a number of advantages to heterogeneous groups. Groups composed of students with diverse backgrounds, abilities, and interests (a) expose students to multiple perspectives and problem-solving methods and (b) generate more cognitive disequilibrium (needed to stimulate students' learning and cognitive development). In heterogeneous groups there tends to be more elaborative thinking, more frequent giving and receiving of explanations, and greater perspective-taking in discussing material, all of which increase the depth of understanding, the quality of reasoning, and the accuracy of long-term retention. To make groups heterogeneous, you assign students to groups using a random or stratified random procedure. Teacher selected groups can be either homogeneous or heterogeneous. When students select their own groups they usually form homogeneous ones. Each of these methods is explained below.

Random Assignment

Perhaps the easiest and most effective way is to assign students to groups randomly. You divide the number of students in your class by the size of the group desired. If you wish to have groups of three and you have thirty students in your class, you divide thirty by three. You have students number off by the result (e.g., ten). Then you have the students with the same number find each other (all one's get together, all two's get together, and so forth). Roger's favorite variation is to have students count off in a different language (e.g., English, Spanish, French, Hungarian) each time you assign them to groups.

Literature Characters

Give students individual cards with the names of characters in the literature they recently have read. Ask them to group with the characters from the same story, play, or poem. Examples include Romeo and Juliet; Captain Hook, Peter Pan and Wendy; and Hansel, Gretel, Ginger-Bread-House Witch, and Step-Mother.

Historical Characters

Give each student a card with the name of a historical character. He or she can then find the other members of their group on the basis of the historical period in which the characters lived. Variations include grouping according to the occupation of the person, country they came from, or significant event or accomplishment.

Math Method

There are endless variations to the math method of assigning students to groups. The basic structure is to give each student a math problem and ask them to (a) solve their problem,

STATES ★ CAPITALS MATCHING LIST

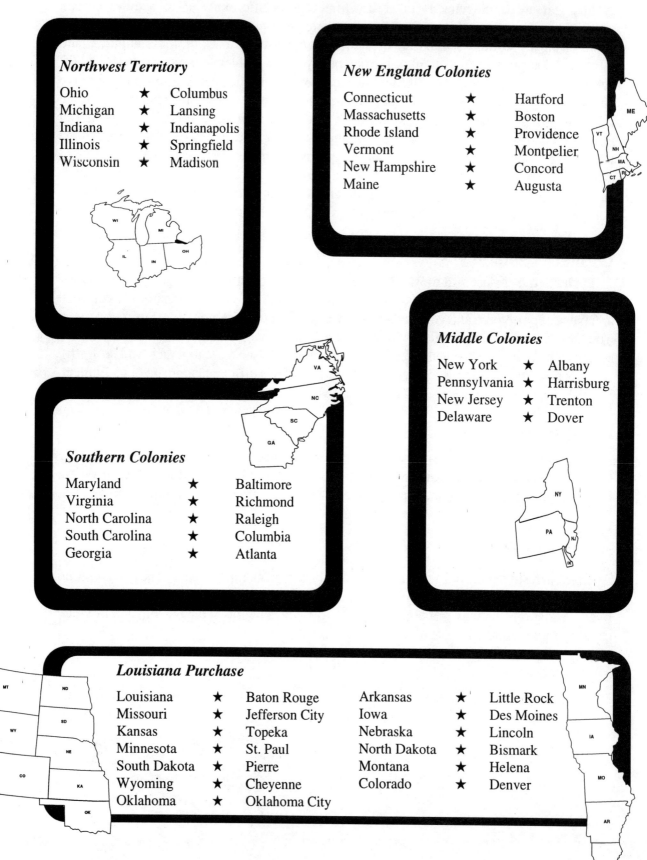

Northwest Territory

Ohio	★	Columbus
Michigan	★	Lansing
Indiana	★	Indianapolis
Illinois	★	Springfield
Wisconsin	★	Madison

New England Colonies

Connecticut	★	Hartford
Massachusetts	★	Boston
Rhode Island	★	Providence
Vermont	★	Montpelier
New Hampshire	★	Concord
Maine	★	Augusta

Southern Colonies

Maryland	★	Baltimore
Virginia	★	Richmond
North Carolina	★	Raleigh
South Carolina	★	Columbia
Georgia	★	Atlanta

Middle Colonies

New York	★	Albany
Pennsylvania	★	Harrisburg
New Jersey	★	Trenton
Delaware	★	Dover

Louisiana Purchase

Louisiana	★	Baton Rouge	Arkansas	★	Little Rock
Missouri	★	Jefferson City	Iowa	★	Des Moines
Kansas	★	Topeka	Nebraska	★	Lincoln
Minnesota	★	St. Paul	North Dakota	★	Bismark
South Dakota	★	Pierre	Montana	★	Helena
Wyoming	★	Cheyenne	Colorado	★	Denver
Oklahoma	★	Oklahoma City			

(b) find the classmates whose problems have the same answer, and (c) form a group. This may vary from simple addition in the first grade to complex equations in high school classes. Thus, to form a group of three, you may distribute the following three equations throughout the class $(3 + 3 = \_)$, $(4 + 2 = \_)$, $(5 + 1 = \_)$.

States and Capitols

To assign students to groups of two or four you may use the following procedure. Divide the number of students in the class by two (30 divided by 2 = 15). Pick a geographic area of the U.S. and write out on cards the names of 15 states. Then on another set of cards write out the names of their capitol cities. Shuffle the cards and pass them out to students. Then have the students find the classmate who has the matching state or capitol. To form groups of four, have two adjacent states and their capitols combine.

Geographical Areas

List a number of countries or states and have students group themselves according to most preferred to visit. Variations include grouping according to least preferred to visit, similar in terms of climate, similar in geological features, having the same exports, and so forth.

Stratified Random Assignment

A related procedure is stratified random assignment. This is the same as random assignment except that you choose one (or two) characteristics of students (such as reading level, learning style, task-orientation, or personal interest) and make sure that one or more students in each group have that characteristic. To assign students to learning groups randomly, stratifying for achievement level, use the following procedure. **First,** rank order students from highest to lowest in terms of a pretest on the unit, a recent past test, past grades, or your best guess as a teacher. **Second,** select the first group by choosing the highest student, the lowest student, and the two middle achievers. Assign them to the group unless they are all of one sex, they do not reflect the ethnic composition of the class, they are worst enemies, or they are best friends. If any of these is true, move up or down one student from the middle to readjust. **Third,** select the remaining groups by repeating the above procedure with the reduced list. If there are students left over, make one or two groups of three members. You may use the same procedure for assigning students to groups of three or two members.

There is a danger in assigning students to groups on the basis of certain characteristics. What categories you use to assign students to groups will give a very loud message to your students as to what characteristics you think are important. If you form groups so that there is a white male, a white female, a black male, and a black female in every group, you are giving the class a clear message that gender and ethnicity are important factors to you as a teacher. Making these categories salient may cue students' stereotypes and prejudices. **The general rule is: If you assign students to groups based on categories, make them unique categories needed to complete the group task** (such as summarizer, creative thinker, time keeper, and library expert). As a teacher, you tell students, "*In your groups there is a creative thinker, a person who is good at keeping track of time, someone who knows how to use the library, and someone who is good at summarizing all the ideas suggested in the group. To complete this assignment, you will need the resources of each member.*" By emphasizing the personal abilities and talents of students rather than their social categories, you focus students on the person, not the social group.

Preferences

Have students write their favorite sport to participate in on a slip of paper. Then have them find groupmates who like to participate in the same sport. Variations include favorite food, celebrity, skill, car, president, animal, vegetable, fairy tale character, and so forth.

Teacher Selected Groups

A third method is teacher selected groups. You can decide who is going to work with whom. You can ensure that nonachievement-oriented students are a minority in each group or that students who trigger disruptive behavior in each other are not together. **One of our favorite methods is creating support groups for each isolated student.** You ask students to list three classmates with whom they would like to work. From their lists, you tally for each student the number of times classmates chose the student. You can then identify the classroom isolates (students who are not chosen by any of their classmates). These are the "at-risk" students who need your help. You take the most socially isolated student and assign two of the most skillful, popular, supportive, and caring students in the class to work with him or her. Then you take the second most isolated student and do the same. In this way you optimize the likelihood that the isolated students will become involved in the learning activities and build positive relationships with classmates. You want to ensure that in your classes, no student is left out, rejected, or believes that he or she does not belong.

Self-Selected Groups

The least recommended procedure is to have students select their own groups. Student-selected groups often are homogeneous with high-achieving students working with other high-achieving students, white students working with other white students, minority students working with other minority students, and males working with other males. Often there is more off-task behavior in student-selected than in teacher-selected groups. A useful modification of the "select your own group" method is to have students list whom they would like to work with and then place them in a learning group with one person they choose and one or two or more students that the teacher selects.

For additional methods for assigning students to groups as well as a variety of team-building and warm-up activities see R. Johnson and Johnson (1985).

Length Of Group Life

A common question teachers often ask is, "*How long should cooperative learning groups stay together?*" The type of cooperative learning group you use determines one answer to this question. Base groups last for at least one and ideally for several years. Informal cooperative learning groups last for only a few minutes or at most one class period.

The question as to how long a cooperative learning group should stay together is a question aimed at formal cooperative learning groups. Actually, there is no formula or simple answer to this question. Some teachers keep cooperative learning groups together for an entire semester or year. Other teachers like to keep a learning group together only long enough to complete a task, unit, or chapter. Our best advice is to allow groups to remain stable long enough for them to be successful. Breaking up groups that are having trouble functioning effectively is often counterproductive as the students do not learn the skills they need to resolve problems in collaborating with each other. **Over the course of a semester or year, however, every student should work with every other classmate.** Each time you form groups, you should **explain to the class that before the year is over, everyone will work in a group with everyone else and, therefore, if they are not in a group with someone they would like to be, do not worry about it. The next group will be different.**

Using Combinations Of Cooperative Learning Groups

In many lessons you will want to use a combination of formal and informal cooperative learning groups as well as base groups. You will use more than one size group in any one lesson. You will need ways to assign students to new groups quickly. You will need procedures for making transitions among groups, moving students from pairs to fours to pairs to threes and so forth. It sometimes helps to have timed drills on how fast students can move from a formal cooperative learning group to an informal pair and then back to their formal group.

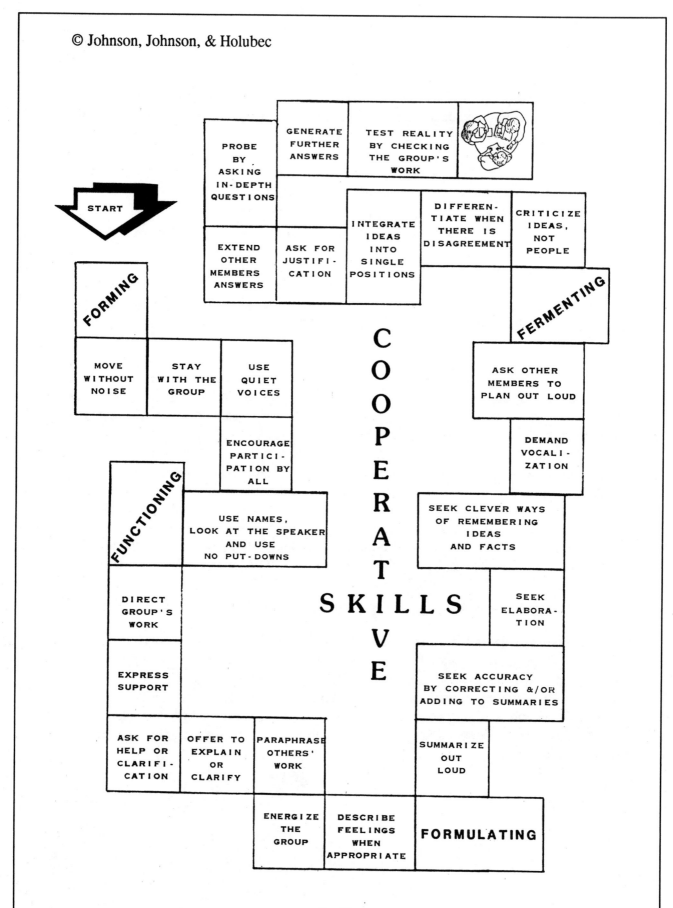

START

PROBE BY ASKING IN-DEPTH QUESTIONS

GENERATE FURTHER ANSWERS

TEST REALITY BY CHECKING THE GROUP'S WORK

EXTEND OTHER MEMBERS ANSWERS

ASK FOR JUSTIFI-CATION

INTEGRATE IDEAS INTO SINGLE POSITIONS

DIFFEREN-TIATE WHEN THERE IS DISAGREEMENT

CRITICIZE IDEAS, NOT PEOPLE

FORMING

FERMENTING

MOVE WITHOUT NOISE

STAY WITH THE GROUP

USE QUIET VOICES

ASK OTHER MEMBERS TO PLAN OUT LOUD

ENCOURAGE PARTICI-PATION BY ALL

DEMAND VOCALI-ZATION

FUNCTIONING

USE NAMES, LOOK AT THE SPEAKER AND USE NO PUT-DOWNS

SEEK CLEVER WAYS OF REMEMBERING IDEAS AND FACTS

C O O P E R A T I V E

S K I L L S

DIRECT GROUP'S WORK

SEEK ELABORA-TION

EXPRESS SUPPORT

SEEK ACCURACY BY CORRECTING &/OR ADDING TO SUMMARIES

ASK FOR HELP OR CLARIFI-CATION

OFFER TO EXPLAIN OR CLARIFY

PARAPHRASE OTHERS' WORK

SUMMARIZE OUT LOUD

ENERGIZE THE GROUP

DESCRIBE FEELINGS WHEN APPROPRIATE

FORMULATING

3 : 10

Chapter Four: Assigning Roles

Throughout Polynesia there is a legend of the great king/god Tiki (son of the sun) who brought his white skinned, bearded, tall people from a far off land in the east about the year 500 AD. In Peru, there is an Inca legend of a white, bearded, tall people who built great stone statues and pyramids, leaving enormous ruins on the shores of Lake Titicaca, but who vanished about 500 AD. They were governed by a high priest and sun-king named Kon-Tiki. Could the Polynesians be descendants from the mysterious tribe who once lived in Peru? Thor Heyerdahl thought so. "*Impossible*," said the authorities,"*the Indians had no ships*!" "*They had rafts made of balsa wood*," argued Heyerdahl. "*Rafts*!" laughed the authorities. *"Sail a raft (constructed exactly as the Indians did so in 500 AD) from Peru 4,500 miles across the roughest ocean in the world to the Polynesian islands, then propose your theory."* So Thor set out to do so. *"We can make it in 100 days easily!"* he told his friends. Five other adventurers agreed to go with him. *"We will call the raft, <u>Kon Tiki</u>,"* decided Thor.

To ensure the success of the expedition, each member was given a role. Herman was given the roles of maintaining the instruments and measuring the currents and winds. Erik was given the roles of patching sails, splicing ropes. and navigating. Knut and Thorstein were given the role of radio operator. Bengt was given the roles of taking scientific notes and quartermaster. Thor was given the roles of captain and keeper of the log book. Everyone took their turn at steering the raft. When high levels of cooperation are called for, it helps to give everyone a specific role. Roles specify who should do what, when, and how. Many times groups will function much more effectively and efficiently when members are assigned specific roles. They began their journey on April 28, 1947. As days wore into weeks and weeks into months, the sturdy raft was battered by high waves and fierce storms, but it always emerged victorious. After 93 days at sea they spotted land! In the distance they saw the island of Puka Puka. The winds, however, were not in their favor and they sailed past the island. During the next several days, they passed a number of islands. On the 101st day of the voyage, they were blown onto a reef off a small Polynesian island. They had made the incredible journey and proved that ancient inhabitants of Peru could indeed have been the first settlers of Polynesia!

Introducing Group Roles

One way to introduce the concept of group roles to your class is by using the analogy of a sports team. List several of the roles on a sports team. In football, for example, the quarterback (who passes or runs the ball) relies on the center (who hikes the ball to the quarterback), guard (who blocks opposing players from tackling the quarterback), and wide receiver (who catches the pass thrown by the quarterback) as well as all the other members of the team. Ask students to explain why it is important for each player to do his or her job and what happens if one or two players do not do their jobs. Then point out that you are going to organize the class into cooperative learning groups and each member will have a key role to perform.

Role	What Happens When A Person Does Not Do His Job?
Center	
Quarterback	
Guard	
Wide Receiver	

Deciding Which Roles To Include In A Lesson

In planning the lesson, you think through what are the actions that need to occur to maximize student learning. **Roles** prescribe what other group members expect from a student (and therefore what the student is obligated to do) and what that person has a right to expect from other group members who have complementary roles. In cooperative groups, roles are often divided into forming, functioning, formulating, and fermenting roles.

Roles That Help The Group Form

Voice Monitor (ensures all group members are using quiet voices).

Noise Monitor (ensures classmates move into groups quietly).

Turn-Taking Monitor (ensures that group members take turns in completing the assignment).

Forming Roles

Roles That Help The Group Function

Roles that help the group achieve its goals and maintain effective working relationships among group members.

☐ **Explainer Of Ideas Or Procedures** (shares one's ideas and opinions).

☐ **Recorder** (writes down the group's decisions and edits the group's report).

☐ **Encourager Of Participation** (ensures that all members are contributing).

☐ **Observer** (records the frequency with which members engage in targeted skills).

☐ **Direction Giver** (gives direction to the group's work by (1) reviewing the instructions and restating the purpose of the assignment, (2) calling attention to the time limits, (3) offering procedures on how to complete the assignment most effectively).

☐ **Support Giver** (gives both verbal and nonverbal support and acceptance through seeking and praising others' ideas and conclusions).

☐ **Clarifier/Paraphraser** (restates what other members have said to understand or clarify a message).

Other examples of roles include **resource roles** where each member is responsible for providing one key piece of information to be incorporated into the group's whole product, **perspective-taking roles** where each member is responsible for contributing one perspective or viewpoint to the group's final product (e.g., ethical, economic, cultural, or global perspective), **cognitive roles** where each member is responsible for contributing one aspect of the critical-thinking process to the group's final product (e.g., analysis, synthesis, evaluation, elaboration, application).

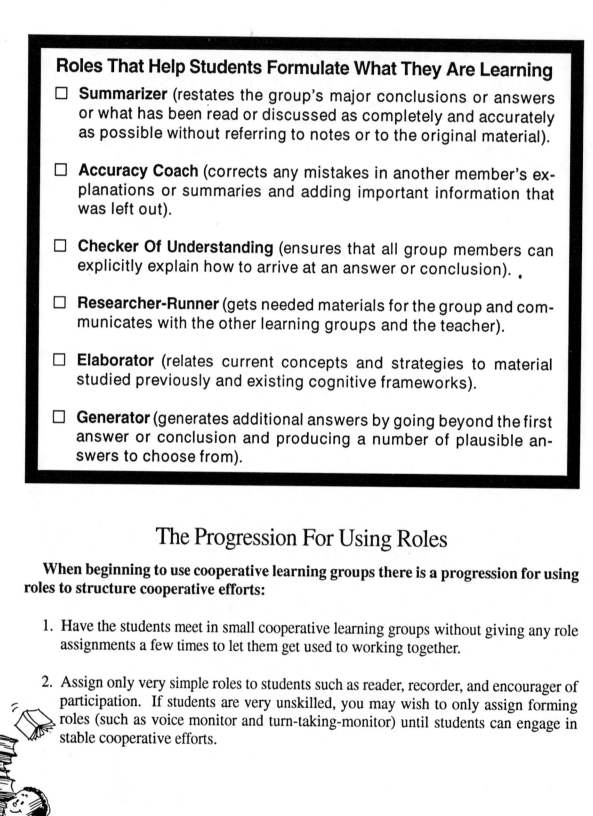

Roles That Help Students Formulate What They Are Learning

☐ **Summarizer** (restates the group's major conclusions or answers or what has been read or discussed as completely and accurately as possible without referring to notes or to the original material).

☐ **Accuracy Coach** (corrects any mistakes in another member's explanations or summaries and adding important information that was left out).

☐ **Checker Of Understanding** (ensures that all group members can explicitly explain how to arrive at an answer or conclusion). .

☐ **Researcher-Runner** (gets needed materials for the group and communicates with the other learning groups and the teacher).

☐ **Elaborator** (relates current concepts and strategies to material studied previously and existing cognitive frameworks).

☐ **Generator** (generates additional answers by going beyond the first answer or conclusion and producing a number of plausible answers to choose from).

The Progression For Using Roles

When beginning to use cooperative learning groups there is a progression for using roles to structure cooperative efforts:

1. Have the students meet in small cooperative learning groups without giving any role assignments a few times to let them get used to working together.

2. Assign only very simple roles to students such as reader, recorder, and encourager of participation. If students are very unskilled, you may wish to only assign forming roles (such as voice monitor and turn-taking-monitor) until students can engage in stable cooperative efforts.

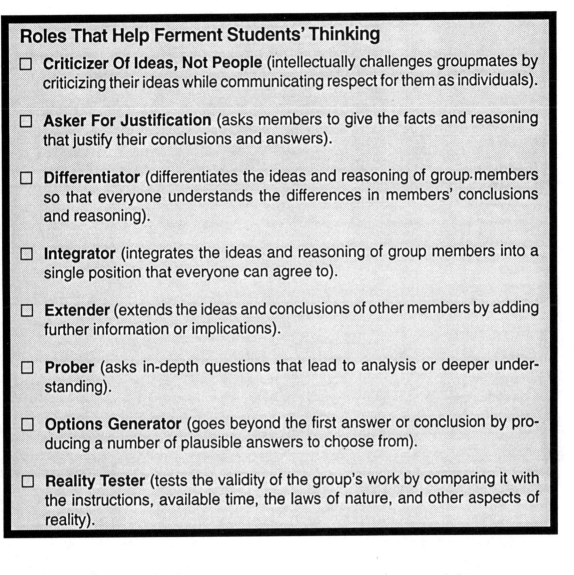

Roles That Help Ferment Students' Thinking

☐ **Criticizer Of Ideas, Not People** (intellectually challenges groupmates by criticizing their ideas while communicating respect for them as individuals).

☐ **Asker For Justification** (asks members to give the facts and reasoning that justify their conclusions and answers).

☐ **Differentiator** (differentiates the ideas and reasoning of group members so that everyone understands the differences in members' conclusions and reasoning).

☐ **Integrator** (integrates the ideas and reasoning of group members into a single position that everyone can agree to).

☐ **Extender** (extends the ideas and conclusions of other members by adding further information or implications).

☐ **Prober** (asks in-depth questions that lead to analysis or deeper understanding).

☐ **Options Generator** (goes beyond the first answer or conclusion by producing a number of plausible answers to choose from).

☐ **Reality Tester** (tests the validity of the group's work by comparing it with the instructions, available time, the laws of nature, and other aspects of reality).

3. Rotate the roles so that each group member plays each one several times.

4. Add a new role periodically that is only slightly more sophisticated, such as checker-for-understanding. Add it to the rotation. You assign the functioning roles at this point.

5. Over time add formulating and fermenting roles that do not occur naturally in the group. Elaborator is an example. Students typically do not relate what they are learning to what they already know until you specifically train them to do so.

Examples Of Roles Appropriate To Each Age Level

Category	Role	Primary	Intermediate	Secondary
Forming	Turn-Taking Monitor	First You, Then Me	Take Turns	Contribute In Sequence
Functioning	Recorder	Writer	Recorder	Scribe
	Encourager of Participation	Say Nice Things	Give Positive Comments	Compliment
	Clarifier/ Paraphraser	Now You Say It	Say It In Your Own Words	Paraphrase
	Consensus Seeker	Everyone Agree	Reach/ Agreement	Reach Consensus
Formulating	Summarizer	Put Together	Combine	Summarize
	Generator	Give Another Answer	Give Additional Answers	Generate Alternative Answers
Fermenting	Asker For Justification	Ask Why	Ask For Reasons	Ask For Justification
	Rationale Giver	Say Why	Give Facts And Reasons	Explain

Making Roles Appropriate To Grade Levels

One of the challenges of using cooperative learning is in describing group roles in an age-appropriate way. How you describe a role to primary students obviously needs to be different from the way you describe the role to high school students. In Table 4.1 are examples of the ways roles are renamed to make them age appropriate.

Sequencing Roles

Roles can be sequenced so that more and more complex and difficult roles are assigned to students each month and each year. Students first need to learn the **forming roles** well. Then leadership skills are taught by assigning students **functioning roles**. The **formulating and fermenting roles** are more complex and need to be taught specifically and directly. It is at this point that cognitive and social roles merge. The social skills represented by the roles should be taught like a spiral curriculum with a more complex version of the skill taught every year.

Solving And Preventing Problems In Working Together

At times there are students who refuse to participate in a cooperative group or who do not understand how to help the group succeed. You can solve and prevent such problems when you give each group member a specific role to play in the group. You assign a role when you give each person a specific job to do, name the job, and specify the actions the member has to take to complete the job. Assigning roles:

1. Reduces problems such as one or more members' making no contribution to the group or one member dominating the group.

2. Ensures that vital group skills are enacted in the group and that group members learn targeted skills.

3. Creates interdependence among group members. You structure **role interdependence** by assigning each member complementary and interconnected roles.

Assigning students roles is one of the most efficient way of ensuring that members work together smoothly and productively.

Using Role Cards

You can construct role cards to help students practice social skills and to understand how to perform their roles and know what to say when taking on a particular role. To construct role cards:

☐ Plan how many groups you will have during the lesson. You will need one set of role cards for each group.

☐ Decide on the roles you will assign to group members. Copy them on cards. One side of the card should have the name of the role. On the other side of the card place phrases the person portraying the role might say. An example of a card is: (side one) checker of understanding and (side two) "Explain to me..., give an example, how did we get that answer, let's review."

☐ Pass out the cards at the beginning of the lesson. You may deliberately assign a role to a particular student. Or you may assign roles randomly, such as letting the color of students' clothes or location in the group determine which role you assign them. Rotate roles regularly so that all students become proficient in each task.

☐ Explain the new roles to students and have students practice them before the group starts work. The cards serve as visuals to supplement your oral explanations. Review the old roles and have students practice them also.

☐ Be creative and think of new roles to assign to your students.

Chapter Five: Arranging the Room

A **labyrinth** is an enclosure containing a network of confusing, intricate, winding pathways that bewilders and confounds all who enter. In Greek legend, such a structure was built by Daedalus for King Minos of Crete, to house the Minotaur (who had the body of a man and the head of a bull). Each year Minos sent seven youths and seven maidens from Athens into the Labyrinth where they wandered until they met the Minotaur, who killed and ate them. There are classrooms like that. To try to get to one side to the other without being distracted from the learning task is a near impossibility.

The design and arrangement of classroom space and furniture are tools that can facilitate or obstruct student learning. You control or at least effect almost all student and teacher behaviors by the way you arrange the classroom. How you arrange your classroom is important for many reasons (see Johnson, 1979):

1. **The physical and spatial aspect of your classroom communicates a symbolic message of what is appropriate behavior and what is expected to happen in the classroom.** The way you arrange the classroom is a message to students. Desks in a row communicate a different message and expectation than desks grouped in small circles.

2. **Classroom design can directly facilitate or interfere with academic achievement.** The way in which interior space is designed influences student achievement and the actual amounts of time students spend on task.

3. **Good spatial definition aids students' visual and auditory focus.** The way in which interior space is designed creates overall visual order and focuses visual attention. It can control acoustics.

4. **Classroom design can directly facilitate or interfere with the learning climate in the classroom.** Good spatial definition can help students feel secure by telling them where the structured learning areas begin and end. The way in which interior space is designed effects the feelings (such as well-being, enjoyment, comfort, anger, and depression) of students and teachers and their general morale.

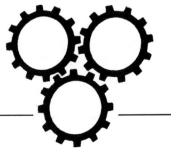

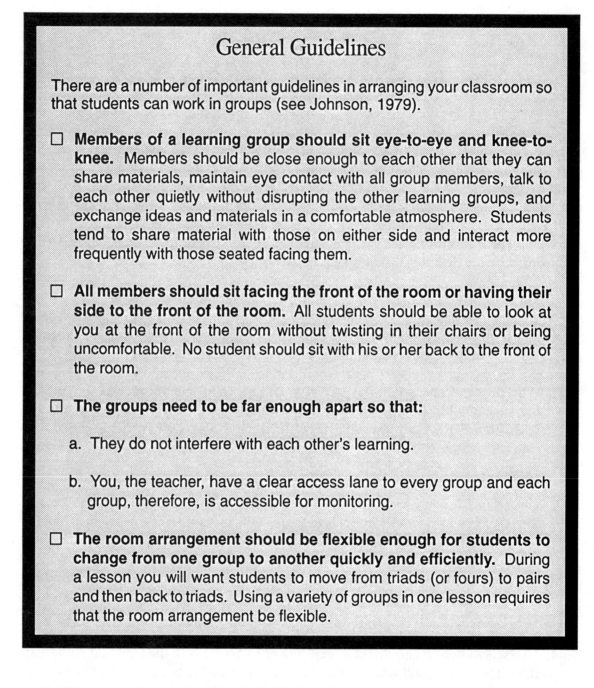

General Guidelines

There are a number of important guidelines in arranging your classroom so that students can work in groups (see Johnson, 1979).

☐ **Members of a learning group should sit eye-to-eye and knee-to-knee.** Members should be close enough to each other that they can share materials, maintain eye contact with all group members, talk to each other quietly without disrupting the other learning groups, and exchange ideas and materials in a comfortable atmosphere. Students tend to share material with those on either side and interact more frequently with those seated facing them.

☐ **All members should sit facing the front of the room or having their side to the front of the room.** All students should be able to look at you at the front of the room without twisting in their chairs or being uncomfortable. No student should sit with his or her back to the front of the room.

☐ **The groups need to be far enough apart so that:**

a. They do not interfere with each other's learning.

b. You, the teacher, have a clear access lane to every group and each group, therefore, is accessible for monitoring.

☐ **The room arrangement should be flexible enough for students to change from one group to another quickly and efficiently.** During a lesson you will want students to move from triads (or fours) to pairs and then back to triads. Using a variety of groups in one lesson requires that the room arrangement be flexible.

5. **Classroom design can directly facilitate or interfere with the classroom management.** Good spatial definition can define circulation patterns in the room. It defines appropriate interaction patterns and guides students work and behavior (thus prevent-

ing some types of discipline problems). The way in which interior space is designed effects the ease of transition from one instruction activity to another.

6. **Classroom design can directly facilitate or interfere with the structure of the learning groups.** The way you design the interior space of your classroom influences the patterns of student (and teacher) participation in instructional activities, the emergence of leadership in the learning groups, and the patterns of communication among students (and between students and teachers).

7. **Classroom design can directly facilitate or interfere with the relationships among students.** The way in which interior space is designed effects the opportunities for social contact among students and the friendship patterns in the class.

Flexible Use Of Space: Defining Work Areas

Since no single classroom arrangement will meet the requirements of all instructional goals and activities, you need to be able to design interior space flexibly. Rearranging your classroom from rows to triads to pairs to fours requires reference points and well-defined boundaries of work spaces.

You visually focus students' attention by using color, form, and lighting. An effective visual environment is an interaction among color, form, and lighting. As a teacher, you can use visual attractions to focus attention on points of emphasis in the classroom (the learning group, you, instructional materials) and define the territorial boundaries of work spaces. You define boundaries by:

1. **Using labels and signs** that designate areas.

2. **Using colors** to attract visual attention and define group and individual spaces as well as different storage areas and resource centers.

3. **Taping lines** on the floor or wall to define the different work areas.

4. **Using forms** such as arrows taped on the wall or hanging from the ceiling to direct attention. You can designate work areas by hanging mobiles from the ceiling. Mobiles can be color-coded. The use of mobiles and displays hanging from the ceiling are underutilized in most classrooms.

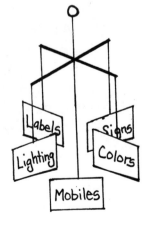

5. **Using lighting** to define specific work areas. Directed light (illuminating part of the room while leaving other areas dim) intensifies and directs students' attention. Brightly lit areas can draw people toward the areas and suggest activity. More dimly lit areas surrounding the lighted ones become area boundaries. As the activity in the classroom changes, the lighting could also change.

6. **Moving furniture** to define work and resource areas. Even tall plants, when placed in pots with wheels, can be moved to provide spatial boundaries.

7. **Displaying group work** to designate work spaces. If a cooperative group is to remain together for a period of several days or weeks, members may wish to build a poster or collage that designates their work area.

You can use many of these same procedures to control acoustically levels of noise in the classroom.

Designing Circulation Patterns

Circulation is the flow of movement into, out of, and within the classroom. It is movement through space. You determine what students see, when they see it, and with whom students interact by the way you design circulation patterns in your classroom. In order for you to use cooperative learning effectively, you need to arrange the classroom to provide for proper circulation patterns. **Students should have easy access to:**

1. Each other.

2. You, the teacher.

3. Materials they need for specific learning assignments.

Environmental Interdependence

You establish environmental interdependence when you arrange the classroom in ways that create the perception that "we sink or swim together." You can bind students together by the way you arrange the classroom. Each group can have a designated area. You can limit the size of group areas by such methods as drawing a circle in masking tape on the floor around the group's meeting area.

Figure 1: Arranging The Classroom

Groups of Three

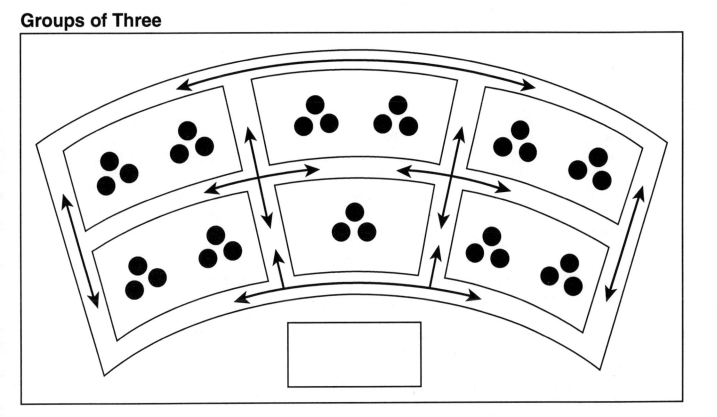

Groups of Three

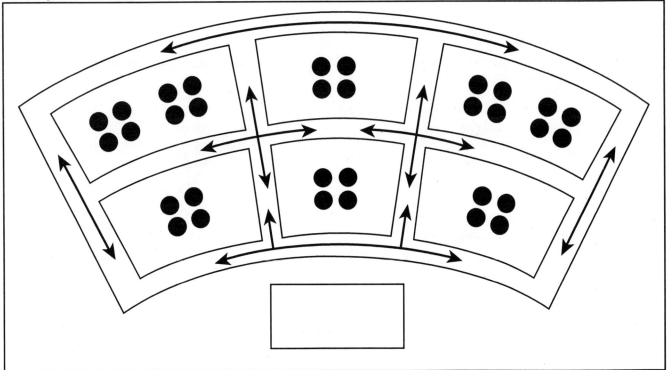

The circulation patterns should allow students to make quick transitions from one grouping to another. Finally, you (the teacher) need to monitor each group carefully during the lesson and, therefore, need easy access to each learning group and each student.

Classroom Arrangement And Discipline Problems

The way you arrange the classroom can increase or decrease the number of discipline problems you have to deal with. Many discipline problems arise in areas of the room that you, the teacher, are not monitoring. Students often misbehave because they believe you are not attending to them and will not notice. By arranging the room in ways that provide you easy access to each group and the ability to monitor the whole classroom easily, you can prevent many discipline problems from developing. Ways to do so with groups of two, three, or four members is illustrated in Figure 1.

Inattentive Students At The Back Of The Room

Beware of the students who want to sit in the back of the room. Keep a special eye on them. Compared to students sitting in the front and middle of the classroom, students who sit in the back of the room tend to contribute less to class discussions, be less attentive, participate less in work related seat tasks, and achieve at a lower level. Low-achieving students whom you move forward tend to achieve more than do low-achieving students who remain in the back of the class. Hostile and alienated students like to sit in the back of the classroom. There is much to be said for keeping students moving around the classroom throughout a class period or lesson so that no one sits at the back of the room too long.

Chapter Six: Planning Instructional Materials

Medusa had once been a beautiful maiden who took great pride in her hair. She even dared to compare herself to the goddess Athena. For such boldness and vanity, Athena changed her into a monster. Her golden ringlets became writhing, twisting snakes. No living thing could gaze on her face without being turned instantly to stone. She was banished to a cave where she lived surrounded by the stone figures of men and animals who had chanced to glimpse her. Perseus, the son of Zeus and Danae, was tricked into volunteering to find the cave and bring back to King Polydectes Medusa's head.

Perseus needed a magic sword, shield, and helmet before he could slay Medusa. Similarly, without the right materials, students cannot complete their assignments. How you distribute materials has important effects on how well students work together to complete assignments. Before the lesson begins you decide what materials are necessary if students are to complete the assigned task and work together cooperatively. Think through what students will have to do to complete the assignment and organize their materials before the lesson begins. Basically, when you use cooperative learning, you use the same curriculum materials you would use if you were teaching the lesson competitively or individualistically. But there are some very interesting things you can do with curriculum materials to increase cooperation among students if you want to. You have seven options.

Planning Instructional Materials

One Per Individual

One Per Group

Combination Individual & Group

Jigsaw of Information

Jigsaw of Equipment & Materials

Intergroup Tournament

First, you can give each student his or her own complete set of materials. Each group member may need a copy of a passage or chapter to read, reread, and refer to while answering questions and making interpretations about its content. Each group member may need his or her own copy of the math problems the group is working to solve. Each group member may need a copy of an atomic chart to refer to easily during the lesson.

Second, you can give each group one set of materials. Limiting the resources given to the group is one way to create positive interdependence among group members. The students have to work together to be successful. This is especially effective the first few times the group meets. Initially, students may tend to work separately if each member has his or her own set of materials. After students become accustomed to working cooperatively, you can give a copy of the materials to each student. One story for two students ensures that they sit side by side and put their heads together. One pencil and paper for two students ensure that they decide when and what to write together. One computer for two or three students ensures that they think through what they are going to do before they use the keyboard and mouse and take action. One microscope for each group ensures that they share experiences and come to consensus about what they observe. Especially when there is not enough equipment for each student, using cooperative learning groups ensures that all students actively utilize the equipment for learning.

Third, you can use a combination of individual and group materials for a lesson. You might give each group member a copy of the story they are reading so he or she can refer to it to answer questions or make interpretations. But you might give the group only one set of questions for the students to answer together as a team.

Fourth, you can make students interdependent by arranging information like a jigsaw puzzle. You give each student part of the information needed to complete the task. Group members are responsible for mastering their information, teaching it to the rest of the group, and learning the information being presented by the other group members. Since each member needs the resources of the other members if he or she is to complete the assignment successfully, resource interdependence exists among group members. You can, for example, give a group the assignment of writing a biography of Abe Lincoln and information on Lincoln's childhood given to one member, information on Lincoln's early political career given to another, information on Lincoln as president given to a third, and information on Lincoln's assassination given to the fourth member. The jigsaw procedure requires every member to participate in order for the group to be successful.

Fifth, you can make students interdependent by arranging equipment and materials like a jigsaw puzzle. In a science class, for example, you can give one student a microscope, one the materials to make a slide, and another a field kit to gather samples. You may give one pair member a pencil, the other pair member a sheet of paper. One student can have a brush, another pair member a set of paints. You may give each group member a different colored pencil. The students are interdependent through the division of the materials they need to complete the assignment.

Jig-Saw Procedure

Task: Think of a reading assignment you will give in the near future. Divide the assignment in three parts. Plan how you will use the jig-saw procedure. Script out exactly what you will say to your class in using each part of the jig-saw procedure.

Procedure: One way to structure positive interdependence among group members is to use the jigsaw method of creating resource interdependence. The steps for structuring a "jigsaw" lesson are:

1. **Cooperative Groups:** Distribute a set of materials to each group. The set needs to be divisible into the number of members of the group (2, 3, or 4 parts). Give each member one part of the set of materials.

2. **Preparation Pairs:** Assign students the cooperative task of meeting with someone else in the class who is a member of another learning group and who has the same section of the material and complete two tasks:

   a. Learning and becoming an expert on their material.

   b. Planning how to teach the material to the other members of their groups.

3. **Practice Pairs:** Assign students the cooperative task of meeting with someone else in the class who is a member of another learning group and who has learned the same material and share ideas as to how the material may best be taught. These "practice pairs" review what each plans to teach their group and how. The best ideas of both are incorporated into each's presentation.

4. **Cooperative Groups:** Assign students the cooperative tasks of:

   a. Teaching their area of expertise to the other group members.

   b. Learning the material being taught by the other members.

5. **Evaluation:** Assess students' degree of mastery of all the material. Reward the groups whose members all reach the preset criterion of excellence.

Sixth, you can have each member make a separate contribution to a joint product. You ask each member, for example, to contribute a sentence to a paragraph, an article to a newsletter, or a chapter to a "book."

Seventh, you can structure materials to create an intergroup competition to compare the level of achievement among the cooperative learning groups. DeVries and Edwards (1973) introduced an intergroup tournament procedure that they called Teams-Games-Tournaments. You assign students to cooperative learning teams heterogeneous in terms of achievement and give the assignment of ensuring that all group members master the assigned material. Group members study together to learn the material. They then participate in a competitive tournament to determine which group learned the material the best. To conduct the tournament you assign each group member to a triad consisting of three students from three different learning groups. The triads are homogeneous in terms of achievement. Members of each triad are at the approximately same achievement level (based on past history). You use a game format for the tournament. The materials required are a set of test questions covering the material learned in the cooperative groups in the center of each triad (each one written on a card), an answer sheet, and a set of procedures and rules. You place a deck of cards in the center of each triad. Students take turns drawing a card and answering the question. If the answer is correct, the student keeps the card. If incorrect, the card is placed on the bottom of the deck. There is a procedure for challenging another student's answer if a triad member believes it is wrong. If the challenger is right, he or she gets the card. The triad member who gets the most cards wins and receives six points, second place receives four points, and last place receives two points. Students take the number of points they won in the tournament triads back to the cooperative learning groups and add the points together. You pronounce the cooperative learning group with the highest number of points the winner.

Ultimately, the choice of materials for a lesson is determined by the type of task and what the students will be doing during the lesson. Imagine how students might work in the group and think about how necessary it would be to see or refer to the materials. When a group is mature and experienced and group members have a high level of interpersonal and small group skills, you may not have to arrange materials in any specific way. But when a group is new or when members are not very skilled, you may wish to distribute materials in carefully planned ways to communicate that the assignment is to be a joint (not an individual) effort.

✳ RULES OF PLAY ✳

A. To start the game shuffle the cards and place them face down on the table. Play is in a clockwise rotation.

B. To play, each player in turn takes the top card from the deck, reads it aloud, and does one of two things:

1. Says he does not know or is not sure of the answer and asks if another player wants to answer. If no one wants to answer, the card is placed on the bottom of the deck. If a player answers, he follows the procedure below.

2. Answers the question immediately and asks if anyone wants to challenge the answer. The player to his right has the first chance to challenge. If he does not wish to challenge, then the player to his right may challenge.

   a. If there is no challenge, another player should check the answer:

      1. If correct, the player keeps the card.

      2. If incorrect, the player must place the card on the bottom of the deck.

   b. If there is a challenge and the challenger decides not to answer, the answer is checked. If the original answer is wrong, the player must place the card on the bottom of the deck.

   c. If there is a challenge and the challenger gives an answer, the answer is checked.

      1. If the challenger is correct, he receives the card.

      2. If the challenger is incorrect, and the original answer is correct, the challenger must give up one of the cards he has already won (if any) and place it on the bottom of the deck.

3. If both answers are incorrect, the card is placed on the bottom of the deck.

C. The game ends when there are no more cards in the deck. The player who has the most cards is the winner.

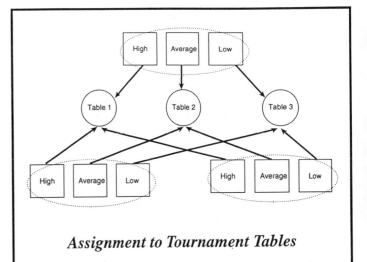

Assignment to Tournament Tables

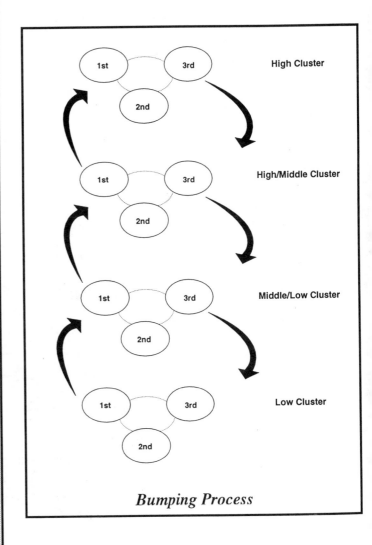

Bumping Process

The Difficult Group

There are a number of difficulties you may avoid by the careful arrangement of instructional materials. There are a number of problem behaviors that you can solve by the arrangement of materials. Some examples are:

1. **The uninvolved group member.** When one or more students do not participate in the group's work, you can assure their involvement by jigsawing the information or materials. You then give each student a specific set of resources to contribute to the groups' work. Giving each member a different colored pen, for example, makes it possible to determine each member's level of involvement.

2. **The domineering group member.** When one student dominates the group discussion, you can define his or her involvement more strictly by jigsawing the information and materials.

3. **Members seated too far apart to work together.** Giving one set of materials to the whole group requires members to sit close together.

Famous Cooperative Groups

Almost every evening, either I went to Braque's studio or Braque came to mine. Each of us **had** to see what the other had done during the day. We criticized each other's work. A canvas wasn't finished unless both of us felt it was. Pablo Picasso (in a letter to Francoise Gilot)

The things Picasso and I said to one another during those years will never be said again, and even if they were, no one would understand them anymore. It was like being roped together on a mountain. Georges Braque

...the noise could be heard all over the city. Our fights over words were furious, blasphemous, and frequent, but even in their hottest moments we both knew that we were arguing academically and not personally. Richard Rodgers (recalling his work with lyricist Larry Hart)

I couldn't have done it without the boys. Casey Stengel (after winning his ninth American League pennant in ten years)

Collaboration operates through a process in which the successful intellectual achievements of one person arouse the intellectual passions and enthusiasms of others, and through a process in which a fact that was at first expressed by only one individual becomes a common intellectual possession instead of fading away into isolation. Alexander Humboldt

Nothing new that is really interesting comes without collaboration. James Watson, Nobel Prize Winner (codiscoverer of the double helix)

Our...advantage was that we had evolved unstated but fruitful methods of collaboration...If either of us suggested a new idea, the other, while taking it seriously, would attempt to demolish it in a candid but nonhostile manner. Francis Crick, Nobel Prize Winner (codiscoverer of the double helix)

The reason we were so good, and continued to be so good, was because he (Joe Paterno) forces you to develop an inner love among the players. It is much harder to give up on your buddy, than it is to give up on your coach. I really believe that over the years the teams I played on were almost unbeatable in tight situations. When we needed to get that six inches we got it because of our love for each other. Our camaraderie existed because of the kind of coach and kind of person Joe was. Dr. David Joyner

Section Three: Explaining Task And Cooperative Structure

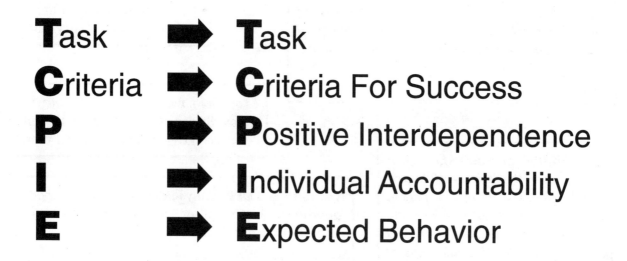

Task	➡	**T**ask
Criteria	➡	**C**riteria For Success
P	➡	**P**ositive Interdependence
I	➡	**I**ndividual Accountability
E	➡	**E**xpected Behavior

Chapter Seven: Explaining Academic Task

At this point you have planned your lesson by specifying the instructional objectives and making all the preinstructional decisions and preparations. The next step is to face your class and inform them of (a) what to do to complete the assignment and (b) how to do it. You explain the academic task so that your students are clear about the assignment and understand the objectives of the lesson. **First, you explain what the assignment is.** The assignment needs to be a clear, measurable task. Students have to know what they are supposed to do--*"Your task is to read the story and answer the questions correctly."* You have to be able to measure whether students have completed the assignment successfully. One advantage of cooperative learning groups is that students who do not understand what they are to do can clarify the assignment and the procedures with each other before asking the teacher.

Second, you explain the objectives of the lesson to ensure maximum transfer and retention. The objectives are sometimes given as outcomes--*"At the end of this lesson you will be able to explain the causes of the French and Indian War."* Explaining the intended outcomes of the lesson increases the likelihood that students will focus on the relevant concepts and information throughout the lesson.

Third, you (a) explain the concepts, principles, and strategies students need to use during the lesson and (b) relate the concepts and information to be studied to students' past experience and learning. Define the relevant concepts. Answer any questions students have about the concepts or facts they are to learn or apply in the lesson. Give examples to help students understand what they are to learn and do in completing the assignment.

Explaining Academic Task

Explain Academic Assignment

Task

Objectives

Concepts, Principles, Strategies

Procedures

Explain Criterion For Success

Create An Expectation Set

Focused Discussion Pairs

Advanced Preparation Pairs

Question And Answer Pairs

Fourth, you explain the procedures students are to follow in completing the assignment. Procedures for how the group members will work together also need to be clear. If you merely tell students to work together, students will determine for themselves what "*working together*" means. To maximize learning, you must inform students of what procedures they should use throughout the lesson. An example of a procedure for the task of "**read the passage and answer the questions**" is:

1. The reader reads the passage aloud while the other two members of the group read silently and listen. The listeners correct anything that is read incorrectly.

2. The first question is read:

   a. Each student gives his or her opinion as to the answer.

   b. The recorder ensures that at least three good answers are generated.

   c. The group decides which answer they like the best.

   d. The checker-for-understanding asks one or more members to explain why the answer selected is the best answer.

3. Step 2 is repeated for each question.

4. After all questions have been answered, the group summarizes:

   a. Their overall view of the passage and what it means.

   b. How what they have learned relates to their previous knowledge about the topic.

Fifth, it is often helpful to ask class members specific questions to check their understanding of the assignment. Such questioning ensures thorough two-way communication, that you effectively gave the assignment, and that students are ready to begin work. You may use a focused discussion to help students organize in advance what they know about the content to be studied and to set students' expectations about the lesson.

Sixth, you ask the groups to generate a visible product that each member can sign. Having to generate a visible product keeps group members on task and increases the likelihood that they will behave responsibly.

Visual Organizers

In explaining the task to students, it is helpful to provide a visual structure to organize their responses. **Visual organizers** are blank illustrations using lines, arrows, boxes, and circles intended to show concrete relationships between abstract ideas or events. Visual organizers guide students' thinking by providing a relevant spatial format to contain their thoughts. They can increase student participation. They provide a direction and purpose for students who may tend to falter when given only verbal instructions or an abstract discussion question. The visual organizer used should match the thinking process required by the activity. You can display the visual organizer on an overhead projector or board and ask students to copy it or you can make one copy for each student or group. You then need to explain to students how to use the visual organizer. A quick demonstration often helps. Some examples of visual organizers are as follows.

Web Networks And Mind Maps

A **web network** is a wheel in which a main idea, important fact, or conclusion is in the center, with supporting ideas and information radiating from it. The purpose of the web network is to organize and clarify what students know about a concept. In the center of the wheel, for example, students may place the concept "*law of gravity.*" Radiating from the center, the students then write down words and phrases that describe the law of gravity. The web network may be taken one step further and used as a tool for organizing and clarifying relationships among concepts. Students do this by constructing a mind map. A **mind map** is an expanded web network that has four major features: (a) key idea, (b) sub-ideas, (c) supporting ideas, and (d) connectors that show relationships.

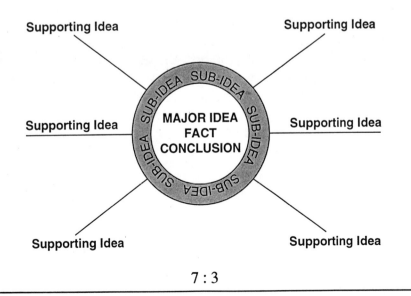

The Continuum

You have students use a **continuum** for tasks that require a ranking or ordering according to given criteria. A science class could use a continuum to rank the life spans of various animals, birds, or insects. You would give them a list of animals and a blank continuum and ask students to rank the animals' life spans from longest to shortest. You could follow this up with asking students to rank the quality of each animal's life from highest to lowest. Students specify the criteria for quality of life. Then they rank each animal according to those criteria.

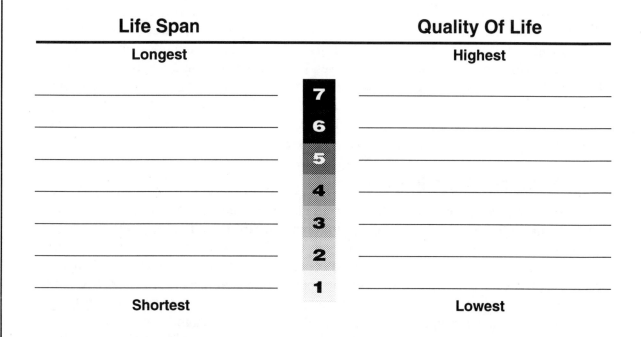

Life Span	Quality Of Life
Longest	Highest

(7, 6, 5, 4, 3, 2, 1)

| Shortest | Lowest |

The Chain Diagram

When you want students to record stages of a process or steps in a procedure, you present them with a **chain diagram**. You could give students the steps in teaching a skill. Then you could present them with a series of behaviors and ask them to classify each according to the step it belongs in. The stages of evolution, the steps in baking a cake, the procedure for driving a golf ball and many, many other things can all be put in chain diagrams to give students a visual organizer for what they are learning.

Teaching A Skill

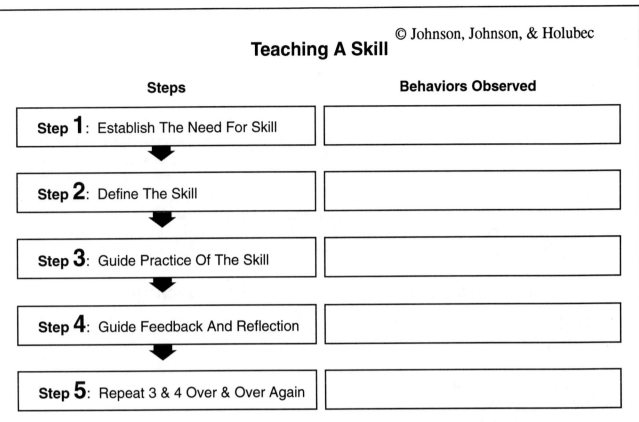

Steps	Behaviors Observed
Step 1: Establish The Need For Skill	
Step 2: Define The Skill	
Step 3: Guide Practice Of The Skill	
Step 4: Guide Feedback And Reflection	
Step 5: Repeat 3 & 4 Over & Over Again	

The Spider Diagram

You have students use a spider diagram when the task is to create supporting details for a central idea. You give students a central idea, such as black holes in the universe, and have them generate a set of categories on which to evaluate it. Under each category they list their ideas. You may, for example, ask students to focus on the effects of polluting the oceans. The group may decide to use the criteria of economic, environmental, political, and miscellaneous effects. Under each criterion students list relevant factors.

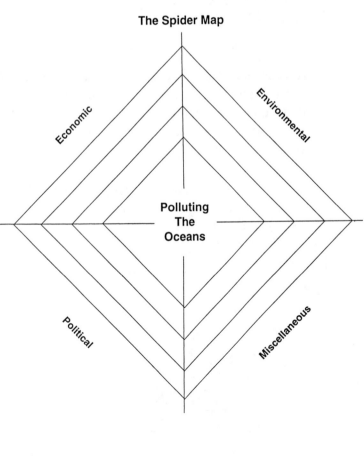

The Chart

You may use a chart to have students formulate a conclusion and then justify it with specific facts. Students can use charts to compare or contrast ideas, events, styles, or people in any subject area. You could, for example, give your students the task of making three critical decisions leading up to the Revolutionary War. To do so they must (a) research each position, (b) formulate a personal decision based on the information they gather, and (c) justify the quality of the decision by referencing the facts. This format of asking for judgments and justification can be applied in a wide range of academic subject areas and disciplines. Students can evaluate any historical or literary event by this method.

Chart 1: Decisions Leading Up To The Revolutionary War

Decision Made	Student Decision	Justification
Boston Tea Party		
Demonstration Leading To Boston Massacre		
Armed Resistance At Lexington And Concord		

Another form of this procedure is to have students evaluate historical figures. Have students examine primary and secondary resources on the individuals being studied. Students then give each leader a "grade" on the basis of the criteria specified. After using such a chart several times, students will be able to generate their own criteria to evaluate historical or literature figures.

Chart Two: Comparison Of Historical Figures

Teddy Roosevelt	Grade	Reasons
Issues Focused On		
Leadership		
Personal Values		

Other Visual Representations

There are other visual ways students can use to organize their work. How to use outlines, Venn diagrams, hierarchies, and causal diagrams are covered in Johnson and Johnson (1992).

Explaining Criteria for Success

While explaining to students the academic task they are to complete, you need to communicate the level of performance you expect of students. Cooperative learning requires criterion-based evaluation. **Criterion-referenced or categorical judgments** are made by adopting a fixed set of standards and judging the achievement of each student against these standards. Making a criterion-referenced judgment is judging what each student can and cannot do. Every student who can achieve up to the standard passes, and every student who cannot fails. A common version of criterion-referenced grading involves assigning letter grades on the basis of the percentage of test items answered correctly. You assign letter grades on the percentage of test items answered correctly.

Sometimes you may wish to set improvement (doing better this week than one did last week) as the criterion of excellence. To promote intergroup cooperation, you may also set criteria for the whole class to reach, such as saying, "*If we as a class can score over 520 words correct on our vocabulary test, each student will receive two bonus points.*"

Grade	Percentage Correct
A	95 - 100
B	85 - 94
C	75 - 84
D	65 - 74
F	Less than 64

Creating An Expectation Set About The Lesson

At the beginning of the lesson you may wish students to meet in pairs or triads to (a) establish expectations about what the lesson will focus on and (b) organize in advance what they know about the topic. Three ways of creating an expectation set and advance organizing are:

1. Focused Discussion Pairs.

2. Advanced Preparation Papers.

3. Question and Answer Pairs.

Focused Discussion Pairs

At the beginning of a lesson, you can use focused discussion pairs to help students (a) cognitively organize in advance what they know about the content to be studied and (b) set expectations about the lesson. You, the teacher, prepare one to three questions that are the focus of the lesson. You ask students to turn to the person nearest them and form a pair. You assign the task of answering the questions. You create a cooperative structure by telling students to create a joint answer to each question by following the formulate, share, listen, create format:

1. Each student formulates his or her answer.

2. Students share their answer with their partner.

3. Students listen carefully to their partner's answer.

4. Pairs create a new answer that is superior to each member's initial formulation through the processes of association, building on each there's thoughts, and synthesizing.

To ensure individual accountability choose one member of several pairs to explain his or hers pair's answer to each question.

Preparation Papers

To prepare for each lesson, you ask students to complete a short writing assignment. Even if you do not grade the papers, it compels students to organize their thoughts and take some responsibility for the lesson's success.

1. Students' task is to write a short paper (one to two pages) on an aspect of the assigned readings to prepare for class. Before each lesson (class session) students:

   a. Choose a major theory, concept, idea, or person discussed in the assigned reading.

b. Write a one to two page analysis of it (1) summarizing the relevant assigned reading and (2) adding material from another relevant source (book, journal, newspaper, magazine) to enrich the analysis.

2. Students meet in their base groups of four members. The base groups stay the same for the entire semester or year. Create the **cooperative structure** by having students bring multiple copies of their paper to class (one for each member of their group and one for you). Each member presents a two to three minute summary of their paper. The members of the cooperative group read, edit, and criticize the paper. They complete an assessment form for each member's paper.

3. Members of each group sign each member's paper. The signature means that they have read the paper and have provided feedback to improve their groupmates' writing skills.

4. The cooperative groups summarize what they have learned from members' papers and how it applies to the topic of the lesson.

Preparation Paper Assessment Form

Points Possible	Criteria	Points Earned
10	Has A Clear, Accurate, Descriptive Title	
10	Begins With A Position Statement	
10	Each Paragraph Is Indented	
10	Each Paragraph Begins With A Topic Sentence	
10	Capitalization, Appearance, Punctuation, Spelling	
10	Includes Information From Two Or More Sources	
10	Includes Persuasive Supporting Sentences	
10	Includes Analysis And Critical Thinking	
10	Ends With Conclusions	
10	Other:	
100	**Total**	

Write specific suggestions on how to improve the paper on the back of this page.

Question And Answer Pairs

1. To prepare for the lesson, students read an assignment and write a set of questions dealing with the major points raised in the assigned reading or other related materials. This results in each student generating a set of test questions for his or her groupmates to answer. You may wish to say, "*Your homework consists of four tasks:*

   a. *Read the assigned material.*

   b. *Choose four major points made by the authors that classmates should understand and remember.*

   c. *For each point write one test question that will challenge your classmates' understanding. Short answer questions that require inference and analysis are ideal.*

   d. *Write out (1) the answer to each question and (2) the page number and paragraph where the answer is found. Do not look for obscure details. Try to write interesting and thought-provoking questions about the major points in the reading assignment.*"

Homework Assignment

	Major Point	Question	Answer	Page #
1				
2				
3				
4				

2. At the beginning of each class, you randomly assign students to pairs (or students can meet in their class base groups). You choose one person (Student A) randomly to ask his or her first question.

3. Their partner (Student B) gives an answer. Student A can correct B's answer or give additional information.

4. Student B now asks Student A a question and they repeat the process.

5. During this time, the teacher goes from dyad to dyad, giving feedback and asking and answering questions.

Chapter Eight: Structuring Positive Interdependence

All for one and one for all.

Alexandre Dumas

Although the sky was clear, the pilot of a chartered flight from Uruguay to Chile miscalculated his position. Rather than descending for his final landing approach, the pilot was actually flying into an extinct volcano, Tinguiririca. Both wings and the tail section were sheared off on impact, and the airplane's fuselage plummeted down the side of the mountain at a speed exceeding 200 miles per hour. It came to rest on the side of a 12,000-foot mountain, surrounded on three sides by other mountain peaks. None of the plane's crew survived long after the crash, but thirty-two of the forty passengers lived. They were trapped in the subzero temperatures of winter in the Andes with only some wine and candy to live on and only with each other to rely on. The survivers were positively interdependent. They realized that no one person could survive on his or her own. Only through the combined efforts of all could the lives of each individual be saved. Such positive interdependence is the heart of cooperative learning.

After explaining the academic task to students, you next create cooperation among students by structuring positive interdependence into the lesson. **Positive interdependence** is linking students together so one cannot succeed unless all group members succeed. Group members have to know that they "*sink or swim together*." It is positive interdependence that requires group members to roll up their sleeves and work together to accomplish something beyond individual success. When students clearly understand positive interdependence, they see that (a) each group member's efforts are required and indispensable for group success (i.e., there can be no "free-riders") and (b) each group member has a unique contribution to make to the joint effort because of his or her resources and/or role and task responsibilities (i.e., there can be no social loafing).

There are two steps in structuring positive interdependence in learning groups:

1. Structure positive goal interdependence.

Positive Goal Interdependence

2. Supplement and strengthen the positive goal interdependence by adding reward/celebration, role, resource, and identity interdependence.

Establishing Positive Goal Interdependence

In every cooperative lesson there has to be positive goal interdependence. In essence, you say to students, *"You have three responsibilities. You are responsible for learning the assigned material. You are responsible for making sure that all other members of your group learn the assigned material. And you are responsible for making sure that all other class members successfully learn the assigned material."* **Positive goal interdependence** unites group members around a common goal--a concrete reason for being. You structure positive goal interdependence by informing group members they are responsible for:

1. **All members scoring above a specified criterion when tested individually**: *"Make sure you score over 90 percent correct on the test and make sure everyone else in your group scores over 90 percent correct on the test."*

2. **All members improving their performance over their previous scores**: *"Make sure each member of your group does better this week than he or she did last week."*

3. **The overall group score (determined by adding the individual scores of members together) being above a specified criterion**: *"Each member of your triad can score up to 100. I will add your individual scores together to make a total group score. That score must be over 270 for you to be successful."*

4. **One product (or set of answers) successfully completed by the group**: *"Each group is to conduct one science experiment and turn in one report that each member has signed to indicate that he or she agrees with the report and can explain what was done, why, and how."*

You structure positive goal interdependence over and over again until both you and your students see it as a natural part of any lesson. Roger's favorite way of highlighting positive goal interdependence is to **require all members to sign the group's product or each other's paper when the work is done.** A student's signature means:

1. I agree with the group's answer.

2. I have mastered the required material and procedures.

POSITIVE INTERDEPENDENCE

TASK
IDENTITY
RESOURCE
ENVIRONMENT
DUTY (ROLE)

FANTASY
REWARD
OUTSIDE ENEMY
GOAL

3. You have my personal word of honor that all other members in this group have mastered the required material and procedures.

Adding Other Types Of Positive Interdependence

When students first begin to work cooperatively, often positive goal interdependence is not enough to ensure cooperation will take place. **You often need to supplement positive goal interdependence with other types of positive interdependence, such as reward/celebration, role, resource, or identity interdependence.** Usually, the more ways you structure positive interdependence in a lesson, the better.

Students' efforts to learn and promote each other's learning need to be (a) observed, (b) recognized, and (c) celebrated. You structure **celebration/reward interdependence** by (a) having group members celebrate their joint success or (b) giving each group member a tangible reward for successfully working together to complete a joint task. Regular **celebrations** of group efforts and success enhance the quality of cooperation. Team celebrations highlight to members that (a) together they have accomplished something beyond what any one member could do, (b) each member's efforts have contributed to the common good (everyone's success, not just his or her own), (c) each member's efforts are appreciated, and (d) each member is respected as an individual. When group members' recognize and respect one's efforts, it builds long-term commitment to achieve.

You may use two types of **tangible rewards** to structure reward interdependence. When all group members achieve up to criterion or when the overall group score reaches criterion, group members may receive:

1. **Academic rewards** (bonus points added to their scores). *"If all group members score above 90 percent on the test, each of you will receive five bonus points."*

2. **Nonacademic rewards** (such as extra free time, extra recess time, stickers, stars, or food). *"If all members of your group score above 90 percent on the test, each of you will receive fifteen extra minutes of recess."*

Occasionally, there is a student who resists taking responsibility for groupmates' learning and behaves as if he or she did not care if the other group members learn or not. This may be time to use a group reward that is particularly attractive to the uncommitted student (as well as to the rest of the group). In one high school class in Los Angeles, we worked with a teacher who was unsuccessful motivating students with all the regular rewards (bonus points, free time, no homework, computer time, and so forth). When we problem-solved

Types of
Positive Interdependence

Positive Goal Interdependence: Students perceive that they can achieve their learning goals if and only if all the members of their group also attain their goals. Members of a learning group have a mutual set of goals that they are all striving to accomplish.

Positive Celebration/Reward Interdependence: Group celebrates success. A joint reward is given for successful group work and members' efforts to achieve.

Positive Resource Interdependence: Each member has only a portion of the information, resources, or materials necessary for the task to be completed and the member's resources have to be combined in order for the group to achieve its goal.

Positive Role Interdependence: Each member is assigned complementary and interconnected roles that specify responsibilities that the group needs in order to complete a joint task.

Positive Identity Interdependence: The group establishes a mutual identity through a name, flag, motto, or song.

Environmental Interdependence: Groups members are bound together by the physical environment in some way. An example is putting people in a specific area in which to work.

Positive Fantasy Interdependence: A task is given that requires members to imagine that they are in a life or death situation and must collaborate in order to survive.

Positive Task Interdependence: A division of labor is created so that the actions of one group member have to be completed if the next team member is to complete his or her responsibility.

Positive Outside Enemy Interdependence: Groups are placed in competition with each other. Group members then feel interdependent as they strive to beat the other groups and win the competition.

with her, she finally decided on offering students "minutes of their own music played in class on Friday" as a group reward. Using the cassette tape recorders from the foreign language lab with several sets of earphones, she was able to reward the groups that earned the reward through good work, while other groups watched as they did (or did not do) their homework. It worked! It is important to match rewards to students, especially the unmotivated students. It is also important to know that **extrinsic rewards should evolve to symbols for celebration and eventually become unnecessary as intrinsic motivation takes over.**

You structure **role interdependence** by assigning each member complementary and interconnected roles (such as reader, recorder, checker of understanding, encourager of participation, and elaborator of knowledge) that specify responsibilities that the group needs in order to complete the joint task. The use of roles is described in Chapter Six. In cooperative groups, you divide responsibilities into roles that help the group to:

1. Form the group and organize it for work.

2. Function effectively (that is, achieve its goals and maintain effective working relationships among members).

3. Formulate what members know and integrate it with what they are learning.

4. Ferment members' thinking to enhance higher-level reasoning.

You structure **resource interdependence** by giving each group member only a portion of the information, materials, or resources necessary for the task to be completed (given that members have to combine their resources to achieve their goals). Ways of structuring resource interdependence include:

1. **Limiting the resources given to the group.** You might give only one pencil, for example, to a group of three students.

2. **Jigsawing information so that each member has part of the information required to complete the assignment.** You give, for example, a group the assignment of writing a biography of Charles Dickens. You give information on Dickens' childhood to one member, information on Dickens' early writing career to another, information on Dickens writing career to a third, and information on Dickens' final years to the fourth member. To complete the assignment the group members have to share their information with their groupmates.

3. **Jigsawing materials so that each member has part of a set of materials.** One student can have crayons, another paper. One student can have the scissors, another paper, and another glue.

4. **Having each member make a separate contribution to a joint product.** You could ask each member, for example, to contribute a sentence to a paragraph, an article to a newsletter, or a chapter to a "book."

You structure **identity interdependence** by having the group establish a mutual identity through a name or a group symbol such as a banner, collage, motto, flag, or song. A shared identity binds members of a group together. You structure **environmental interdependence** by binding group members together through the physical environment in some way (such as a specific area to meet in). You structure **fantasy interdependence** by placing students in hypothetical situations where they are to solve a problem (such as how to deal with being shipwrecked on the moon). You structure **task interdependence** by creating a division of labor so that one group member has to complete his or her actions if the next group member is to complete his or her responsibilities (such as a sample of swamp water has to be gathered before a slide can be made before the sample can be examined under a microscope). You structure **outside enemy interdependence** by creating an intergroup competition in which groups strive to outperform the other groups.

There is no way to overemphasize the importance of strong positive interdependence among group members. It is the glue that holds groups together. It is the source of members' mutual commitment to each other's well-being and success. Without positive interdependence, cooperation does not exist. Structuring positive interdependence is the most important aspect of using cooperative learning groups in your classes.

Structuring Intergroup Cooperation

You can extend the positive outcomes resulting from cooperative learning throughout a whole class by structuring intergroup cooperation. You establish class goals as well as individual and group goals. You may give bonus points to each class member if everyone reaches a preset criterion of excellence. When a group finishes its work, the teacher should encourage the members to (a) find other groups who are finished and compare and explain answers and strategies or (b) find other groups who are not finished and help them understand how to complete the assignment successfully.

Structuring Individual Accountability

What children can do together today, they can do alone tomorrow.

Vygotsky

Among the early settlers of Massachusetts there was a saying, "*If you do not work, you do not eat.*" Everyone had to do his or her fair share of the work. There is no free lunch in a cooperative learning group. A group is not truly cooperative if some members are "slackers" who let others do all the work. A group is not truly cooperative if members tell each other the answers without teaching each other how to get the answers. To be a cooperative group, each member must be held accountable to learn the assigned material and help other group members learn. Individual accountability results in group members knowing they cannot "hitch-hike" on the work of others, loaf, or get a free ride. As one group of middle-school students put it, *"In this chain there will be no weak links!"*

Using cooperative learning includes structuring group and individual accountability. You structure **group accountability** by assessing the overall performance of the group and giving the results back to group members to compare to a standard of performance. You structure **individual accountability** by:

1. Assessing the performance of each individual member.

2. Giving the results back to the individual and the group to compare to a preset standard of performance. The feedback enables members to (a) recognize and celebrate efforts to learn and contributions to groupmates' learning, (b) provide immediate remediation and any needed assistance or encouragement, and (c) reassign responsibilities to avoid any redundant efforts by members.

3. Ensuring group members hold each other responsible for contributing his or her fair share to the group's success.

Individual accountability is the key to ensuring that all group members are in fact strengthened by learning cooperatively. **The purpose of cooperative groups is to make each member a stronger individual in his or her own right.** After participating in a cooperative lesson, group members should be better prepared to complete similar tasks by themselves. There is a pattern to classroom learning. **First,** students learn knowledge, skills, strategies, or procedures in a cooperative group. **Second,** students apply the knowledge or perform the skill, strategy, or procedure alone to demonstrate their personal mastery of the

material. Students learn it together and then perform it alone. Common ways to structure individual accountability include:

1. **Keeping the size of the group small.** The smaller the size of the group, the greater the individual accountability.

2. **Giving an individual test to each student.** This includes practice tests to see who is and is not ready to take an examination.

3. **Giving random individual oral examinations.** You randomly select students to explain answers or present his or her group's work to you (in the presence of the group) or to the entire class.

4. **Observing each group and group member** and recording the frequency with which each member contributes to the group's work.

5. **Assigning one student in each group the role of checker of understanding.** The **checker** asks other group members to explain the reasoning and rationale underlying group answers.

6. **Having students teach what they learned to someone else.** When all students do this, it is called simultaneous explaining.

7. **Having group members edit each other's work.**

8. **Having students use what they have learned to solve a different problem.**

Positive interdependence and individual accountability are interrelated. In cooperative learning groups, members share responsibility for the joint outcome. Each group member takes **personal responsibility** for (a) contributing his or her efforts to accomplish the group's goals and (b) helping other group members do likewise. The greater the positive interdependence structured within a cooperative learning group, the more students will feel personally responsible for contributing their efforts to accomplish the group's goals. The shared responsibility adds the concept of ought to members' motivation--one **ough**t to do one's share, contribute, and pull one's weight. The shared responsibility also makes each group member personally accountable to the other group members. Students will realize that if they fail to do their fair share of the work, other members will be disappointed, hurt, and upset.

Positive Interdependence
Individual Accountability
Group Processing
Social Skills

FACE-to-Face Promotive Interaction

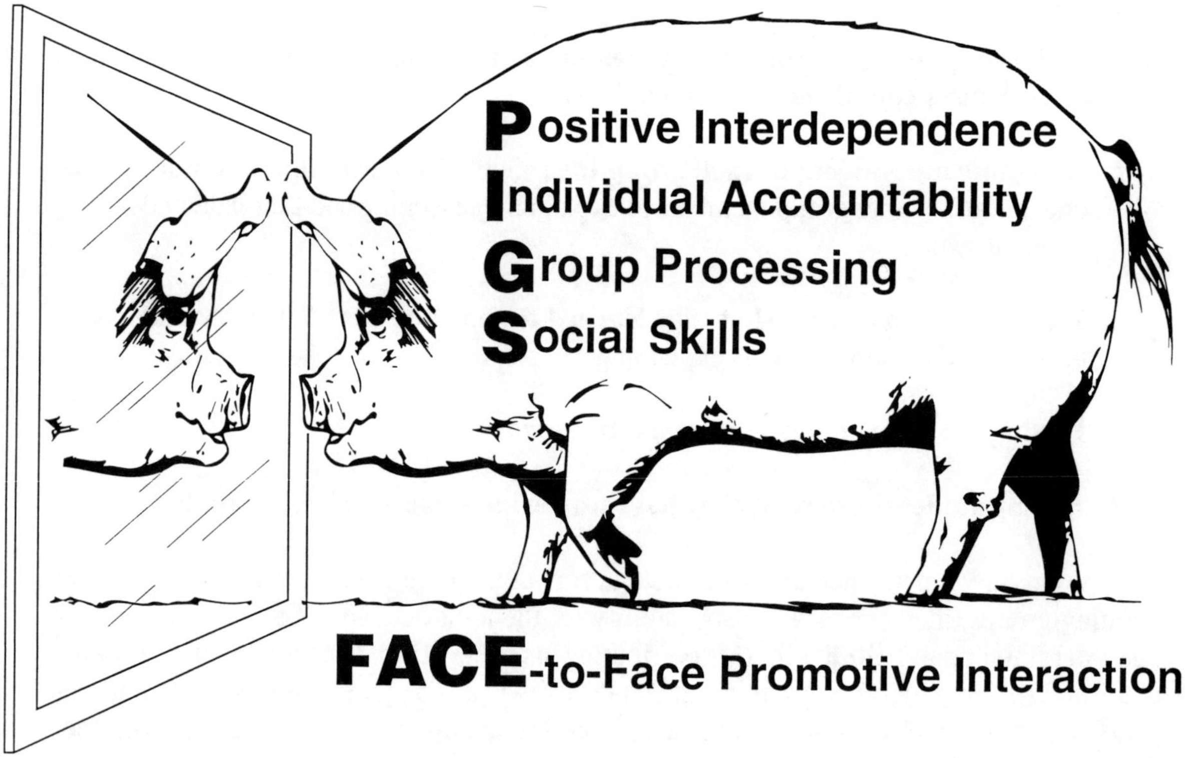

Chapter Nine: Specifying Desired Behaviors

I will pay more for the ability to deal with people than any other ability under the sun.
John D. Rockefeller

Placing socially unskilled students in a group and telling them to cooperate does not guarantee that they are able to do so effectively. We are not born instinctively knowing how to interact effectively with others. Interpersonal and small group skills do not magically appear when they are needed. You must teach students the social skills required for high quality cooperation and motivate students to use the skills if cooperative groups are to be productive.

When you use cooperative learning you must teach students the small group and interpersonal skills they need to work effectively with each other. In cooperative learning groups, students must learn both academic subject matter (**taskwork**) and the interpersonal and small group skills required to function as part of a group (**teamwork**). Cooperative learning is inherently more complex than competitive or individualistic learning because students have to simultaneously engage in taskwork and teamwork. If students do not learn the teamwork skills, then they cannot complete the taskwork. If group members are inept at teamwork, their taskwork will tend to be substandard. On the other hand, the greater the members' teamwork skills, the higher will be the quality and quantity of their learning.

There are two important issues in teaching students the teamwork skills they need to work together cooperatively:

1. What interpersonal and small group skills to teach.

2. How to teach teamwork skills.

When We Work In Groups We:

G   Give Encouragement

R   Respect Others

O   On Task (Stay)

U   Use Quiet Voices

P   Participate Actively

S   Stay In Our Group

Teamwork Skills

What Teamwork Skills To Teach

Numerous interpersonal and small group skills affect the success of cooperative efforts. To coordinate efforts to achieve mutual goals, students must (a) get to know and trust each other, (b) communicate accurately and unambiguously, (c) accept and support each other, and (c) resolve conflicts constructively (Johnson, 1991, 1993; Johnson & F. Johnson, 1994). What cooperative skills you emphasize in a lesson depends on what skills your students have and have not mastered. There are four levels of cooperative skills (see discussion of group roles in Chapter Four):

1. **Forming:** The skills needed to establish a cooperative learning group, such as "stay with your group and do not wander around the room," "use quiet voices," "take turns," and "use each other's names."

2. **Functioning:** The skills needed to manage the group's activities in completing the task and maintaining effective working relationships among members, such as giving one's ideas and conclusions, providing direction to the group's work, and encouraging everyone to participate.

3. **Formulating:** The skills needed to build deeper-level understanding of the material being studied, to stimulate the use of higher-quality reasoning strategies, and to maximize mastery and retention of the assigned material. Examples are explaining step-by-step one's reasoning and relating what is being studied to previous learning.

4. **Fermenting:** The skills needed to stimulate reconceptualization of the material being studied, cognitive conflict, the search for more information, and the communication of the rationale behind one's conclusions. Examples are criticizing ideas (not people) and not changing your mind unless you are logically persuaded (majority rule does not promote learning).

Since the skills in each of these categories were listed in Chapter Four, they are not discussed here.

How To Teach Teamwork Skills

When police evaluate potential suspects, they look for the joint presence of three characteristics: opportunity, motive, and means. Engaging in an interpersonal action requires the contact opportunity with other people for the act to occur, a reason sufficient to motivate the act, and access to a method or procedure whereby the act can occur. For students to work as a team, they need (a) an opportunity to work together cooperatively (where teamwork skills can be manifested), (b) a motivation to engage in the teamwork skills (a reason to believe that such actions will be beneficial to them), and (c) some proficiency in using teamwork skills. After providing students with the opportunity to learn in cooperative groups, you must provide students with the motive and means for doing so.

S Show Need

T T-Chart It

E Engage Students In Practice

R Reflect On Success

N Practice Until Engaging In Skills Is Natural

The first step is to ensure that students see the need for the teamwork skill. To establish the need for the teamwork skill, you can:

1. Ask students to suggest teamwork skills they need to work together more effectively. From the skills suggested, you choose one or more to emphasize in the lesson.

2. Decide what cooperative skills will be emphasized in the lesson and present a case to students that they are better off knowing, than not knowing the skills. Ways to do so are displaying postures, telling students how important the skills are, complementing students who use the skills.

3. Setting up a short role play that provides a counter-example where the skill is obviously missing in a group is a fun way to illustrate the need for the skill.

K Keep On Task

I Include Everyone

S Six-Inch Voices

S Stay With Your Group

The second step is to ensure that students understand what the skill is, how to engage in the skill, and when to use the skill. To give students a clear idea of what the skill is and how and when to perform it, you can:

1. Operationally define the skill into actual verbal and nonverbal behaviors so that students know specifically what to do. It is not enough to tell students what skills you wish to see them use

E Encourage Everyone

S Share Ideas

during the lesson (*"Please encourage each other's participation and check each other's understanding of what is being learned."*). What is encouraging to one student may be discouraging to another. You must explain exactly what they are to do. One way to explain a social skill is through a T-Chart. The teacher lists the skill (e.g., encouraging participation) and then asks the class, *"What would this skill look like (nonverbal behaviors)?"* After students generate several ideas, you ask the class, *"What would this skill sound like (phrases)?"* Students list several ideas. You then display the T-Chart prominently for students to refer to.

Encouraging Participation

Looks Like	Sounds Like
Smiles	What is your idea?
Eye Contact	Awesome!
Thumbs Up	Good idea!
Pat On Back	That's interesting.

2. Demonstrate and model the skill in front of the entire class and explain it step-by-step until your students have a clear idea of what the skill sounds and looks like.

3. Have students role play the skill. You can have each student practice the skill twice in their groups as a role play before the lesson begins.

The third step is to set up practice situations and encourage mastery of the skill. To master a skill, students need to practice it again and again. You can guide their practice by:

1. Assigning the social skill as either a specific role for certain members to fulfill or a general responsibility for all group members to engage in.

2. Observing each group (and utilizing student observers to do likewise) and recording which members are engaging in the skill with what frequency and effectiveness. This is discussed in Chapter 11.

3. Periodically cueing the skill throughout the lesson by asking a group member to demonstrate the skill.

The fourth step is to ensure that each student (a) receives feedback on his or her use of the skill and (b) reflects on how to engage in the skill more effectively next time. Practicing teamwork skills is not enough. Students must receive feedback on how frequently and how well they are using the skill. On the basis of the feedback received and their own assessment of their skill use, the students reflect on how to use the skill more effectively in the future. This is discussed in Chapter 13.

The fifth step is to ensure that students persevere in practicing the skill until the skill seems a natural action. With most skills there is a period of slow learning, then a period of rapid improvement, then a period where performance remains about the same, then another period of rapid improvement, then another plateau, and so forth. Students have to practice teamwork skills long enough to make it through the first few plateaus and integrate the skills into their behavioral repertoires. There are stages most skill development goes through:

1. **Self-conscious, awkward engaging in the skill.**

2. **Feelings of phoniness while engaging in the skill.** After a while the awkwardness passes and enacting the skill becomes more smooth. Many students, however, feel inauthentic or phony while using the skill. Students need teacher and peer encouragement to move through this stage.

3. **Skilled but mechanical use of the skill.**

4. **Automatic, routine use** where students have fully integrated the skill into their behavior repertoire and feel like the skill is a natural action to engage in.

Students should continuously improve their teamwork skills by refining, modifying, and adapting them.

There are three rules for teaching students social skills. **Be specific.** Operationally define each social skill by a T-Chart. **Start small.** Do not overload your students with more social skills than they can learn at one time. One or two behaviors to emphasize for a few lessons is enough. Students need to know what behavior is appropriate and desirable within a cooperative learning group, but they should not be subjected to information overload. **Emphasize overlearning.** Having students practice skills once or twice is not enough. Keep emphasizing a skill until the students have integrated it into their behavioral repertoires and do it automatically and habitually.

Checking For Understanding

Looks Like	Sounds Like
Eye contact	Explain that to me please.
Leaning forward	Can you show me?
Interested expression	Tell us how to do it.
Open gestures and posture	How do you get that answer?
	Give me an example please.
	How would you explain it to the teacher?

Contributing Ideas

Looks Like	*Sounds Like*
Leaning forward	My idea is...
Open gestures and posture	I suggest...
Taking turns	We could...
One person talking with others listening	I suggest we...
	This is what I would do.
	What if we...

Summarizing

Looks Like	Sounds Like
Leaning forward	Let's review what we have said.
Pleasant expression	Our key ideas seem to be...
Open gestures and postures	At this point, we have...
	The points we have made so far are...

Teaching Teamwork Skills

Steps In Teaching A Skill	Teacher Actions
Step 1: **Establish The Need For The Skill**	1. Students choose needed skills. 2. You choose and explain. 3. Role play the absence of the skill.
Step 2: **Define The Skill**	1. Define with T-chart. 2. Demonstrate, model, explain.
Step 3: **Guide Practice Of The Skill**	1. Assign the social skill as a role. 2. Record frequency and quality of use. 3. Periodically cue the skill. 4. Intervene to clarify. 5. Coach.
Step 4: **Guide Feedback And Reflection**	1. Report data to class, group, individuals. 2. Chart/graft the data. 3. Have students analyze/reflect on the data. 4. Ensure every student receives positive feedback. 5. Have students set improvement goals. 6. Have groups celebrate their hard work.
Step 5: **Repeat Steps 3 And 4 Repeatedly**	Emphasize continuous improvement while proceeding through the steps of skill development over and over again.

Section Four: Conducting The Lesson, Monitoring, And Intervening

M 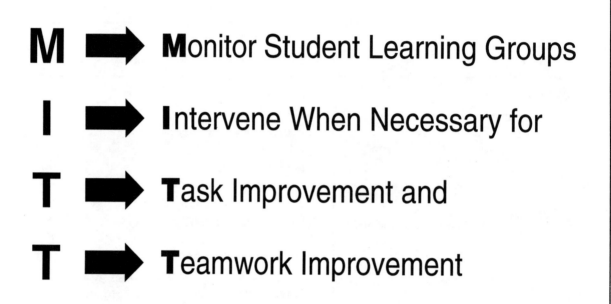 **M**onitor Student Learning Groups

I **I**ntervene When Necessary for

T **T**ask Improvement and

T **T**eamwork Improvement

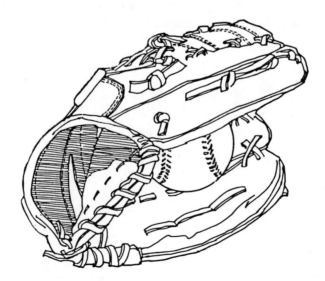

Chapter Ten: The Cooperative Lesson

During the lesson students work together to complete the assignment. Using cooperative learning effectively is an art based on engineering lessons so that they include the five basic elements. There are, however, standard procedures that can be used over and over again that provide a pattern and flow to classroom life. Completing an assignment, for example, can involve taking complete and accurate notes, summarizing what is being learned periodically throughout the lesson, reading assigned material, and writing compositions. Students do so through the following cooperative procedures:

1. Cooperative note taking pairs.

2. Turn to your neighbor discussions.

3. Read and explain pairs.

4. Cooperative writing and editing pairs.

5. Drill and review pairs.

6. Academic controversies.

Cooperative Note-Taking Pairs

The notes students take during a lesson are important in understanding what a student learns, both during the lesson and during reviews of the lesson. Most students, however, take notes very incompletely because of low working memory capacities, the information processing load required, and lack of skills in note taking. Students can benefit from learning how to take better notes and how to review notes more effectively.

1. You assign students to note-taking pairs. The **task** is to focus on increasing the quantity and quality of the notes taken during a lesson. The **cooperative goal** is for both students to generate a comprehensive set of accurate notes that will enable them to learn and review the material covered in the lesson.

2. Every ten minutes or so, you stop the lesson and have students share their notes. Student A summarizes his or her notes to Student B. Student B summarizes his or her notes to Student A. Each pair member must take something from their partner's notes to improve his or her own notes.

Turn-To-Your-Neighbor Summaries

A common practice in most classrooms is to hold a "whole-class discussion." You choose one student or a student volunteers to answer a question or provide a summary of what the lesson has covered so far. The student doing the explaining has an opportunity to clarify and extend what he or she knows through being actively involved in the learning process. The rest of the class is passive. You (the teacher) may ensure that all students are actively learning (and no one is passive) by requiring all students to explain their answers or to summarize simultaneously through the formulate, share, listen, and create procedure.

1. The task for students is to explain their answers and reasoning to a classmate and practice the skill of explaining. The cooperative goal is to create a joint answer that both members agree to and can explain.

2. **Students formulate an answer to a question** that requires them to summarize what the lesson has covered so far.

3. Students turn to a neighbor (classmate close by) and share their answers and reasoning.

4. **Students listen carefully to their partner's explanation.**

5. **Students create a new answer that is superior to their initial formulations** through the processes of association, building on each other's thoughts, and synthesizing.

6. The teacher monitors the pairs and assists students in following the procedure. To ensure individual accountability, you may wish to ask randomly selected students to explain the joint answer they created with their partner.

Formulate, Share, Listen, Create

Read And Explain Pairs

Whenever you give material to students to read, students may read it more effectively in cooperative pairs than individually.

1. Assign students to pairs (one high reader and one low reader in each pair). Tell them what specific pages you wish them to read. The **expected criterion for success** is that both members must be able to explain the meaning of the assigned material correctly.

2. The **task** is to learn the material being read by establishing the meaning of each paragraph and integrating the meaning of the paragraphs into the meaning of the assigned material as a whole. The **cooperative goal** is for both members to agree on the meaning of each paragraph, formulate a joint summary, and be able to explain its meaning to the teacher.

3. The **procedure** the student pairs follow is:

   a. Read all the section headings to get an overview.

   b. Both students silently read the first paragraph. Student A is initially the **summarizer** and Student B is the **accuracy checker**. Students rotate the roles after each paragraph.

   c. The **summarizer** summarizes in his or her own words the content of the paragraph to his or her partner.

   d. The **accuracy checker** listens carefully, corrects any misstatements, and adds anything that was left out. He or she relates the material to something they already know.

   e. The students move on to the next paragraph, switch roles, and repeat the procedure. They continue until they have read all the assignment. They summarize and agree on the overall meaning of the assigned material.

4. During the lesson the teacher systematically (a) **monitors** each reading pair and assists students in following the procedure, (b) ensures **individual accountability** by randomly asking students to summarize what they have read so far, and (c) reminds students that there is **intergroup cooperation** (whenever it is helpful they are to check procedures, answers, and strategies with another group or compare answers with those of another group if they finish early.

Reading Comprehension Triads

Tasks:

1. Read the (poem, chapter, story, handout) and answer the questions.
2. Practice the skill of checking.

Cooperative:

1. One set of answers from the group, everyone has to agree, everyone has to be able to explain each answer.
2. If all members score 90 percent or better on the test, each member will receive 5 bonus points.
3. To facilitate the group's work, each member is assigned a role: Reader, recorder, checker.

Expected Criteria For Success: Everyone must be able to answer each question correctly.

Individual Accountability:

1. One member from your group will be randomly chosen to explain the group's answers.
2. A test will be given on the assigned reading that each member takes individually.
3. Each group member will be required to explain the group's answers to a member of another group.

Expected Behaviors: Active participating, checking, encouraging, and elaborating by all members.

Intergroup Cooperation: Whenever it is helpful, check procedures, answers, and strategies with another group. When you are finished, compare your answers with those of another group and discuss.

Jigsaw Procedure

Whenever there is material you wish to present to a class or you wish students to read, the jigsaw method is an alternative to lecture and individual reading. You assign students to cooperative groups, give all groups the same topic, and take the material and divide it into parts like a jigsaw puzzle so that each student has part of the materials needed to complete the assignment. You give each member one unique section of the topic to learn and then teach to the other members of the group. Members study the topic and teach their part to the rest of the group. The group synthesizes the presentations of the members into the whole picture. In studying the life of Sojourner Truth (a black abolitionist and women's rights activist), for example, you give one student material on Truth's childhood, another material on her middle life, and another material on the final years of her life. Group members, therefore, cannot learn her total life unless all members teach their parts. In a jigsaw each student then has to participate actively in order for his or her group to be successful. The **task** for students is to learn all the assigned material. The **cooperative goal** is for each member to ensure that everyone in their group learn all the assigned material. The **Jigsaw Procedure** is as follows:

1. **Cooperative Groups:** Assign students to cooperative groups (you usually use groups of three, but you may jigsaw materials for groups of any size). Distribute a set of materials to each group so that each group gets one part of the materials. The set needs to be divisible into the number of members of the group. Number each part (Part 1, Part 2, Part 3).

2. **Preparation Pairs:** Ask students to form a preparation pair with a member of another group who has the same part they do (a pair of Part 1's, a pair of Part 2's, a pair of Part 3's). Students have two tasks:

   a. Learning and becoming an expert on their part of the lesson materials.

   b. Planning how to teach their part of the material to the other members of their groups.

   Students are to read their part of the material together, using the pair reading procedure of (a) both students silently read each paragraph (or "chunk"), (b) one student summarizes its meaning while the other student checks the summary for accuracy, and (c) the students reverse roles after each paragraph. In doing so pair members should list the major points they wish to teach, list practical advice related to major points, prepare a visual aid to help them teach the content, and prepare procedures to make the other members of their group active, not passive, learners. The **cooperative goal** is to create one teaching plan

for the two members that both members are able to teach. Both members need their individual copy of the plan.

3. **Practice Pairs:** Ask students to form a practice pair with a member of another group who has the same part they do but who was in a different preparation pair. The **tasks** are for the members to practice teaching their part of the assigned material, listening carefully the their partner's practice, and incorporating the best ideas from the other's presentation into their own. The **cooperative goal** is to ensure that both members are practiced and ready to teach.

4. **Cooperative Groups:** Students return to their cooperative groups. Their tasks are to:

   a. Teach their area of expertise to the other group members.

   b. Learn the material being taught by the other members.

   The **cooperative goal** is to ensure that members master all parts of the assigned material.

5. **Monitoring:** While the pairs and the cooperative groups work, you systematically move from group to group and assist students in following the procedures.

6. **Evaluation:** Assess students' degree of mastery of all the material by giving a test on all the material that students take individually. You may wish to give members of groups whose members all score 90 percent or above five bonus points.

Drill-Review Pairs

There are times during a lesson that you may wish to have students review what they have previously learned and drill on certain procedures to ensure that they are overlearned. When you do so, cooperative learning is indispensable.

Task: Correctly solve the problems or engage in the procedures.

Cooperative Goal: The mutual goal is to ensure that both pair members understand the strategies and procedures required to solve the problems correctly. The teacher assigns two roles: Explainer (explains step-by-step how to solve the problem) and accuracy checker (verifies that the explanation is accurate, encourages, and provides coaching if needed). Students rotate the two roles after each problem.

Individual Accountability: The teacher randomly chooses one member to explain how to solve a randomly selected problem.

Procedure: Assign students to pairs. Assign each pair to a foursome. Implement the following procedure:

1. Person A reads the problem and explains step-by-step the procedures and strategies required to solve it. Person B checks the accuracy of the solution and provides encouragement and coaching.

2. Person B solves the second problem, describing step-by-step the procedures and strategies required to solve it. Person A checks the accuracy of the solution and provides encouragement and coaching.

3. When the pair completes two problems, members check their answers with another pair. If they do not agree, they resolve the problem until there is consensus about the answer. If they do agree, they thank each other and continue work in their pairs.

4. The procedure continues until students complete all the problems.

Cooperative Writing and Editing Pairs

When your lesson includes students writing an essay, report, poem, story, or review of what they have read, you should use cooperative writing and editing pairs.

Tasks: Write a composition and edit other students' compositions.

Criteria For Success: A well-written composition by each student. Depending on the instructional objectives, the compositions may be evaluated for grammar, punctuation, organization, content, or other criteria set by the teacher.

Cooperative Goal: All group members must verify that each member's composition is perfect according to the criteria set by the teacher. Students receive an individual score on the quality of their compositions. You can also give a group score based on the total number of errors made by the pair (the number of errors in their composition plus the number of errors in their partner's composition).

Individual Accountability: Each student writes his or her own composition.

Procedure:

1. The teacher assigns students to pairs with at least one good reader in each pair.

2. Student A describes to Student B what he or she is planning to write. Student B listens carefully, probes with a set of questions, and outlines Student A's composition. The written outline is given to Student A.

3. This procedure is reversed with Student B describing what he or she is going to write and Student A listening and completing an outline of Student B's composition, which is then given to Student B.

4. The students research individualistically the material they need to write their compositions, keeping an eye out for material useful to their partner.

5. The two students work together to write the first paragraph of each composition to ensure that they both have a clear start on their compositions.

6. The students write their compositions individualistically.

7. When completed, the students proofread each other's compositions, making corrections in capitalization, punctuation, spelling, language usage, topic sentence usage, and other aspects of writing specified by the teacher. Students also give each other suggestions for revision.

8. The students revise their compositions, making all of the suggested revisions.

9. The two students then reread each other's compositions and sign their names (indicating that they guarantee that no errors exist in the composition).

While the students work, the teacher monitors the pairs, intervening where appropriate to help students master the needed writing and cooperative skills. When students complete their compositions, students discuss how effectively they worked together (listing the specific actions they engaged in to help each other), plan what behaviors they are going to emphasize in the next writing pair, and thank each other for the help and assistance received.

Academic Controversies

Creating intellectual conflict (controversy) to improve academic learning is one of the most powerful and important instructional tools at teachers' disposal (Johnson & Johnson, 1992). Academic controversies require a cooperative context and are actually an advanced form of cooperative learning. The basic format for structuring academic controversies is:

1. Choose a topic that has content manageable by the students and on which at least two well-documented positions (pro and con) can be prepared. Organize the instructional materials into pro and con packets. Students need to know what their position is and where to find relevant information so they can build the rationale underlying the pro or con position on the issue.

2. Assign students to groups of four. Divide each group into two pairs. Assign pro and con positions to the pairs. A good reader or researcher should be in each pair.

3. Assign each pair the **tasks** of (a) learning its position and the supporting arguments and information, (b) researching all information relevant to its position (giving the opposing pair any information found supporting the opposing position), (c) preparing a series of persuasive arguments to support its position, and (d) preparing a persuasive presentation to be given to the opposing pair. Give students the following instructions:

"Plan with your partner how to advocate your position effectively. Read the materials supporting your position. Find more information in the library reference books to support your position. Plan a persuasive presentation. Make sure you and your partner master the information supporting your assigned position and present it in a persuasive and complete way so that the other group members will comprehend and learn the information."

4. Highlight the **cooperative goals** of reaching a consensus on the issue, mastering all the information relevant to both sides of the issue (measure by a test taken individually), and writing a quality group report on which all members will be evaluated. Note that each group member will receive five bonus points if all members score 90 percent or better on the test covering both sides of the issue.

5. Having each pair present its position to the other. Presentations should involve more than one media and

persuasively advocate the "best case" for the position. There is no arguing during this time. Students should listen carefully to the opposing position and take notes. You tell students:

"As a pair, present your position forcefully and persuasively. Listen carefully and learn the opposing position. Take notes, and clarify anything you do not understand."

6. Having students openly discuss the issue by freely exchanging their information and ideas. For higher-level reasoning and critical thinking to occur, it is necessary to probe and push each other's conclusions. Students ask for data to support each other's statements, clarify rationales, and show why their position is a rationale one. Students evaluate critically the opposing position and its rationale, defend their own positions, and compare the strengths and weaknesses of the two positions. Students refute the claims being made by the opposing pair, and rebut the attacks on their own position. Students are to follow the specific rules for constructive controversy. Students should also take careful notes on and thoroughly learn the opposing position. Sometimes a *"time-out"* period needs to be provided so that pairs can caucus and prepare new arguments. Teachers encourage more spirited arguing, take sides when a pair is in trouble, play devil's advocate, ask one group to observe another group engaging in a spirited argument, and generally stir up the discussions.

"Argue forcefully and persuasively for your position, presenting as many facts as you can to support your point of view. Listen critically to the opposing pair's position, asking them for the facts that support their viewpoint, and then present counter-arguments. Remember this is a complex issue, and you need to know both sides to write a good report."

7. Have the pairs reverse perspectives and positions by presenting the opposing position as sincerely and forcefully as they can. It helps to have the pairs change chairs. They can use their own notes, but may not see the materials developed by the opposing pair. Students' instructions are:

"Working as a pair, present the opposing pair's position as if you were they. Be as sincere and forceful as you can. Add any new facts you know. Elaborate their position by relating it to other information you have previously learned."

8. Have the group members drop their advocacy and reach a decision by consensus. Then they:

a. Write a group report that includes their joint position and the supporting evidence and rationale. Often the resulting position is a third perspective or synthesis that is more rational than the two assigned. All group members sign the report indicating that they agree with it, can explain its content, and consider it ready to be evaluated.

b. Take a test on both positions individually. If all group members score above the preset criteria of excellence (90 percent), each receives five bonus points.

You can find a more detailed description of conducting academic controversies in Johnson and Johnson (1992). Peggy Tiffany, a 4th-grade teacher in Wilmington, Vermont, regularly conducts an academic controversy on whether the wolf should be a protected species. She gives students the cooperative assignment of writing a report on the wolf in which they summarize what they have learned about the wolf and recommend the procedures they think are best for regulating wolf populations and preserving wolves within the continental United States. She randomly assigns students to groups of four, ensuring that both male and female and high-, medium-, and low-achieving students are all in the same group. She divides the group into two pairs and assigns one pair the position of an environmental organization that believes wolves should be a protected species and assigns the other pair the position of farmers and ranchers who believe that wolves should not be a protected species.

Ms. Tiffany gives each side a packet of articles, stories, and information that supports their position. During the first class period each pair develops their position and plans how to present the best case possible to the other pair. Near the end of the period pairs are encouraged to compare notes with pairs from other groups who represent the same position. During the second class period each pair makes their presentation. Each member of the pair has to participate in the presentation. Members of the opposing pair take notes and listen carefully. During the third class period the group discusses the issue following a set of rules to help them criticize ideas without criticizing people, differentiate the two positions, and assess the degree of evidence and logic supporting each position. During the first half of

the fourth hour the pairs reverse perspectives and present each other's positions. Students drop their advocacy positions, clarify their understanding of each other's information and rationale and begin work on their group report. Students spend the first half of the fifth period finalizing their report. You evaluate the report on the quality of the writing, the evaluation of opinion and evidence, and the oral presentation of the report to the class. The students then take an individual test on the wolf and, if every member of the group achieves up to criterion, they all receive the bonus points. Finally, during the sixth class period each group makes a 10-minute presentation to the entire class summarizing their report. All four members of the group need to participate orally in the presentation.

Within this lesson you structure positive interdependence by (a) having each group arrive at a consensus, submit one written report, and make one presentation; (b) jigsawing the materials to the pairs within the group; and (c) giving bonus points if all group members score well on the test. You structure individual accountability by having (a) each member of the pair orally participating in each step of the controversy procedure, (b) each member of the group orally participating in the group presentation, and (c) each member taking an individual test on the material. The social skills emphasized are those involved in systematically advocating an intellectual position and evaluating and criticizing the position advocated by others, as well as the skills involved in synthesis and consensual decision making. Students derive numerous academic and social benefits from participating in such structured controversies (Johnson & Johnson, 1992a).

Joint Project

Joint Project

Task: Complete a project.

Cooperative: Each group completes one project. Members sign the project to indicate that they have contributed their share of the work, that they agree with its content, and they can present/explain it. When a variety of materials are used (such as scissors, paper, glue, markers), assign each team member a responsibility for one of the materials. If appropriate, assign each group member a specific role.

Criteria For Success: A completed project that each group member can explain/present.

Individual Accountability:

1. Each group member may be given different color pens, markers, or pencils.

2. Each group member presents the group project to a member of another group.

3. Each student takes a test individually on the content covered by the project.

Expected Social Skills: Presenting ideas, eliciting ideas, and organizing work.

Ingroup Cooperation: Whenever it is helpful, check procedures, information, and progress with other groups.

Examples:

1. Using compass readings, draw a treasure map for another group to follow.

2. Make a list of the reasons for not growing up (*Peter Pan* by J. M. Barrie).

Chapter Eleven: Monitoring Students' Behavior

The only thing that endures over time is the law of the farm: I must prepare the ground, put in the seed, cultivate it, water it, then gradually nurture growth and development to full maturity...there is no quick fix.

Stephen Covey

Your academic and social skills objectives demand that you assess students' academic and teamwork efforts. You do so during the lesson. Your job begins in earnest when the cooperative learning groups start working. Resist that urge to get a cup of coffee or grade papers. Instead, you move from group to group systematically monitoring students as they work together. You observe the interaction among group members to assess students' (a) academic progress and (b) appropriate use of interpersonal and small group skills. You are responsible for listening to each group and collecting data on the interaction among group members. Based on your observations, you intervene to improve students' taskwork and teamwork. Remember, **students respect what we inspect**.

To **monitor** means to check continuously. **Monitoring has four stages:**

1. **Preparing for observing** the learning groups by deciding who will be the observers, what observation forms to use, and training the observers.

2. **Observing** to assess the quality of cooperative efforts in the learning groups.

3. **Intervening when it is necessary** to improve a group's taskwork or teamwork.

4. **Having students assess the quality of their own individual participation** in the learning groups to encourage self-monitoring.

Five Minute Walk

1. Select social skill(s) to observe.

2. Construct observation sheet.

3. Plan route through the classroom.

4. Gather data on every group.

5. Feedback the data to the groups and/or to the class as a whole.

6. Chart / graph the results.

Preparing For Observing

To prepare for observing you decide who will be the observers, decide what observation forms to use, and train the observers. **Observation** is aimed at recording and describing members' behavior as it occurs in the group. Its **purpose** is to provide objective data about the interaction among group members. You observe the behavior of group members so that (a) you can give them feedback about their participation in the group and (b) they can analyze the group's effectiveness.

Deciding On Observers

1. **The Teacher:** You, the teacher, are always an observer. In every lesson, you systematically roam from group to group. You gather specific information on the interaction of members in each group. When necessary, you intervene to improve group members' taskwork and/or teamwork.

2. **Students:** When students become experienced in working in cooperative learning groups, you train them to be observers. Students may be roving observers who circulate throughout the classroom and monitor all learning groups. Similar to the teacher, student roving observers need a sampling plan to ensure that they observe all groups an approximately equal amount of time. Students may also observe their own groups (one observer per group). In this case, student observers remove themselves slightly from the group so they are close enough to see and hear the interaction among group members but are not tempted to participate in the academic task. Observers do not comment or intervene while the group is working. You set aside a time near the end of the class period for the learning groups to review the content of the lesson with the observer. The role of observer rotates so that each member is an observer an equal amount of time.

3. **Visitors:** Visitors should not be allowed to sit and watch a lesson passively. When someone visits your classroom, hand them an observation form, explain the role of the observer, and put them to work. Visitors may be roving observers or they may observe one single group, depending on the purpose of their visit.

4. **The Sampling Plan For Roving Observers:** Before the lesson begins you plan how much time you will spend observing each learning group (this is a **sampling plan**). You may observe one learning group for the entire class period, collecting information on every member. Or, if the class period lasts for 50 minutes and there are ten groups in the class, you may decide to observe each group for five minutes. Or, you may observe each group for two minutes and rotate through all the groups twice during one class period. You interrupt the sampling plan if you need to intervene in one group.

Cooperative Learning: Classroom Observation

Teacher:_____ Date:_____ Observer: _____

Teacher Actions	Implementation	Comments
Objectives	❏ Academics ❏ Social Skills	
Positive Interdependence	❏ Group Goal ❏ Group Celebration/Reward ❏ Resources Shared/Jigsawed ❏ Roles Assigned ❏ Shared Identity	
Group Composition	❏ Random ❏ Teacher Selected	
Seating Arrangement	❏ Clear View/Access to Groupmates, Teacher ❏ Clear View/Access to Materials	
Individual Accountability	❏ Each Student Tested Individually ❏ Students Check Each Other ❏ Random Student Evaluated ❏ Role: Checker for Understanding	
Define Social Skills	❏ Define (T-Chart) ❏ Demonstrate/Model ❏ Guided Practice ❏ Assign As Role	
Observation Of Taskwork And Teamwork	❏ Teacher Monitors And Intervenes ❏ Students Monitor ❏ Formal Observation Form ❏ Informal (Anecdotal) Observation	
Teacher Feedback: Teamwork Skills	❏ Class ❏ Group ❏ Individual ❏ Frequency And Quality Of Use ❏ Charts and Graphs Used ❏ Positive Feedback To Each Student	
Group Processing	❏ Analysis/Reflection: Teamwork & Taskwork ❏ Goal Setting For Improvement ❏ Celebration	
General Climate	❏ Group Products Displayed ❏ Group Progress Displayed ❏ Aids To Group Work Displayed	

Deciding On Observation Forms

Observation procedures may be **structured or formal** (using an observation schedule on which frequencies are tallied) or **unstructured or anecdotal** (making informal descriptions of students' statements and actions). In both structured and unstructured observation, it is important not to confuse observation with inferences and interpretations. **Observation is descriptive, inferences are interpretative.** Observation involves recording what students do while they work together to complete a task. On the basis of the observation data, inferences and interpretations are made about how well the students are cooperating.

Making Structured Observations

1. Decide which teamwork and taskwork skills you will observe.

2. Construct an observation form to record the frequencies of targeted actions. If students are going to be observers, the form must be appropriate for their age group.

3. Observe each group and record on the observation sheet how often each student performs the specified behaviors.

4. Summarize your observations in a clear and useful manner such as plotting them in a chart or graft.

Using Observation Forms

Observation forms are useful tools for gathering and sharing specific information on how group members work together while completing an assignment.

1. Write the names of group members across the top of the form's columns, placing one name above each column (reserving the first column for the targeted skills and the last column for the row totals).

2. Write the names of the targeted skills in the first column, giving each skill one row.

3. Use one observation form for each group. Place a tally mark in the appropriate row and column when a student engages in one of the targeted actions. Do not worry about recording everything, but observe as accurately and rapidly as possible.

4. Make notes on the back of the observation form if something occurs that should be shared with the group but does not fit into the actions being observed.

Observation Form

Observer:_____ Date:_____ Group: _____

Actions	Edythe	Keith	Dale	Total
Contributes Ideas				
Encourages Participation				
Checks For Understanding				
Gives Group Direction				
Other:				
Total				

5. Write down specific positive contributions by each group member (to ensure that every member will receive positive feedback).

6. Look for patterns of behavior in the group.

7. After the work session is over, total the columns and rows. You may wish to summarize the results in a chart or graft.

Anecdotal Observations

Observer:_____ Date:_____

Note 1:   Group:_____ Student(s):_____

Note 2:   Group:_____ Student(s):_____

Note 3:   Group:_____ Student(s):_____

Note 4:   Group:_____ Student(s):_____

8. Show the observation form to the group, holding it so every group member can see it. Ask the group, "*What do you conclude about:*

   a. Your participation in the group?

   b. The group functioning in general?"

   Ensure all group members receive positive feedback about their efforts to learn and help their groupmates learn.

9. Help the group set a growth goal. Ask, "*What could you add to be even a better group tomorrow than you were today?*" Emphasize the continuous improvement of group effectiveness.

10. Transfer the totals to long-term record sheets and the appropriate charts or graphs.

Observation forms are sometimes called check sheets because they are used to answer the question, "*How often are certain events or actions happening?*" **Structured observation forms** help a group tally and count the number of times an event is observed in a specified time period. You design the form so that all potential observers can use it.

Creating A Structured Observation Form

1. Define exactly what events or actions are being observed (all observers have to be looking for the same thing). The number of skills you choose to focus on determines the number of rows you will have in the observation form (plus one more row for the column totals).

2. Determine the time period during which you will collect the information (minutes to weeks). Usually, the observation form is used for one class session.

3. Enter the social skills to be observed in the first column (each social skill is placed in a separate row, the final row is reserved for the total of each of the other columns).

4. Write the names of group members above the columns (each group member's name is placed above a separate column, the final column is reserved for the row totals).

5. Make sure all columns and rows are clearly labeled and there is enough space to enter data.

You make **unstructured observations** by recording significant, specific events involving students working together cooperatively. You "eavesdrop" on each group and make specific observations that are (a) brief enough to write down quickly, (b) capture an important aspect of the behavior of one or more students, and (c) provide help in answering questions about the successful implementation of cooperative learning. Write positive incidents on cards and file them under the student's name (after they have been used to give the student feedback). You can then access the cards in parent conferences as examples of the student's competencies and positive qualities.

Observing

Guideline One: Use a formal observation sheet to count the number of times students engage in the targeted behaviors. The more concrete the data, the more useful it is to you and your students. A variety of observation instruments and procedures that you can use for these purposes are in Johnson and Johnson (1993).

Guideline Two: Try not to count too many different behaviors at one time. You may wish to choose two to four behaviors from our observation sheet to record the first few times you observe. Once you have used the observation sheet several dozen times, you will be able to keep track of all the behaviors included.

Checklist

Behavior	Yes	No	Comments
1. Do students understand the task?			
2. Have students accepted the positive interdependence & individual accountability?			
3. Are students working toward the criteria, and are those criteria appropriate?			
4. Are students practicing the specified behaviors, or not?			

Guideline Three: Sometimes you may use a simple checklist in addition to a systematic observation form. An example of the checklist is given below.

Guideline Four: Focus on positive behaviors. Celebrated their occurrence. Discuss "why" when they are absent.

Guideline Five: Supplement and extend the frequency data with notes on specific student actions. Especially useful are skillful interchanges that you observe and can share with students later as objective praise. You can also share them with parents in conferences or telephone conversations.

Guideline Six: Train students to be observers. Student observers can obtain more complete data on each group's functioning. For very young students you must keep the system very simple, perhaps only "*Who talks?*" Many teachers have had good success with student observers, even in kindergarten. One of the more important things for you to do is to give the class adequate instructions (and perhaps practice) on gathering the observation data and sharing it with the group. The observer is in the best position to learn about the skills of working in a group. We can remember one first grade teacher who had a student who talked all the time (even to himself while working alone). He tended to dominate any group he was in. When she introduced student observers to the class, she made him an observer. One important rule for observers was not to interfere in the task but to gather data without talking. He was gathering data on who talks and he did a good job, noticing that one student had done quite a bit of talking in the group whereas another had talked very little. The next day when he was a group member, and there was another observer, he was seen starting to talk, clamping his hand over his mouth and glancing at the observer. He knew what was being observed for and he didn't want to be the only one with marks. The teacher said he may have listened for the first time in the year. So the observer often benefits in learning about group skills.

Mystery Person

1. Inform the class that you will be focusing on one student whose name will be kept secret.

2. Select a student randomly or select a student who will be a positive role model or who could benefit from some recognition.

3. Observe during the lesson without showing whom you are observing.

4. Describe to the whole class what the person did (frequency data) without naming the person.

5. Ask students to guess who the mystery person is.

Guideline Seven: When you use student observers, allocate several minutes at the end of each group session for the group to teach the observer what members of the group have just learned. Often important changes are made during this review.

Guideline Eight: You may wish to use cooperative learning enough so that students understand what it is and how they should behave in helping each other learn before introducing student observers. Whether or not you use student observers, however, you should always monitor cooperative learning groups while they work.

Intervening In Cooperative Learning Groups

On the basis of your observations, you intervene to facilitate a group's taskwork or teamwork.

Providing Task Assistance

Systematically observing cooperative learning groups provides you with a "window" into students' minds. Listening to students explain how to solve a problem or complete the assignment to groupmates provides better information about what students do and do not know and understand than do correct answers on tests or homework assignments. Listening in on students' explanations provides valuable information about how well the students understand the instructions, the major concepts and strategies being learned, and the basics of working together effectively. Through working cooperatively students make hidden thinking processes overt and subject to observation and commentary. You are able to observe how students are constructing their understanding of the assigned material and intervene when necessary to help students understand what they are studying.

In monitoring the groups as they work, you will wish to clarify instructions, review important procedures and strategies for completing the assignment, answer questions, and teach task skills as necessary. In discussing the concepts and information to be learned, you will wish to use the language or terms relevant to the learning. Instead of saying, *"Yes, that is right,"* you will wish to say something more specific to the assignment, such as, *"Yes, that is one way to find the main idea of a paragraph."* The use of the more specific statement reinforces the desired learning and promotes positive transfer by helping the students associate a term with their learning.

One way to intervene is to interview a cooperative learning group. You can ask group members a set of questions that requires them to analyze their plan of action at a metacognitive level and explain it to you. Three standard questions are:

1. What are you doing?

2. Why are you doing it?

3. How will it help you?

Intervening In Cooperative Learning Groups

O = Observe

IDQ = Intervene by sharing data and/or asking a question.

SP = Have students process and make three plans for solving the problem.

BTW = Tell students to go back to work.

Intervening In Cooperative Learning Groups

Nonverbal	Verbal
S = Smiles	Close Your Books, Pencils Down, Look At Me
O = Open Gestures	I've Noticed That...
F = Forward Leaning	Explain What My Observation Sheet Shows
T = Touch	What Is Our Social Skills Goal?
T = Tonality	What Are Three Plans For Solving Problem?
E = Eye Contact	I Will Observe You Later To See If Your Plan Is Working.
N = Nodding Head	Open Your Books, Get Back To Work.

Intervening to Teach Teamwork Skills

Cooperative learning groups provide you with a picture of students' social skills. The social skills required for productive group work, along with activities that you may use in teaching them, are covered in Johnson and F. Johnson (1994) and Johnson (1991, 1993). You monitor students' teamwork skills for three reasons:

1. To find students who do not have the necessary social skills to be effective and positive group members and help them learn, improve, and refine their teamwork skills.

2. To find disruptive and ineffective patterns of interaction among group members and teach the teamwork skills necessary to eliminate the disruptive patterns and replace them with constructive patterns of interaction.

3. To find *"good news opportunities"* by:

    a. Giving students the opportunity to use teamwork skills to facilitate their own and each other's learning.

    b. *"Catching them in the act."*

    c. Publicly recognizing the effective actions with positive feedback.

    d. Celebrating the student's (or students') contributions to the group's work.

Ideas For Monitoring And Intervening

Check For	If Present	If Absent
Members seated closely together	*Good seating.*	Move your chairs closer together
Group has right materials and are on right page	*Good, you are all ready.*	Get what you need--I will watch.
Students who are assigned roles are doing them	*Good! You're doing your jobs.*	Who is supposed to do what?
Groups have started task	*Good! You've started.*	Let me see you get started. Do you need any help?
Cooperative skills being used (in general)	*Good group! Keep up the good work!*	What skills would help here? What should you be doing?
A specific cooperative skill being used	*Good encouraging! Good paraphrasing!*	Ask Edye for her ideas. Repeat in your own words what Edye just said.
Academic work being done well	*You are following the procedure for this assignment. Good group!*	You need more extensive answers. Let me explain how to do this again.
Members ensuring individual accountability	*You're making sure everyone understands. Good work!*	Roger, explain why the group chose this answer.
Reluctant students involved	*I'm glad to see everyone participating.*	I'm going to ask Helen to explain #4. Get her ready; I will be back.
Members explaining to each other what they are learning and their reasoning processes	*Great explanations! Keep it up.*	I want each of you to take a problem and explain to me step-by-step how to solve it.
Group wanting to compete with the other groups.	*I'm glad you're helping the other groups. Good citizenship!*	Each of you go to another group and share your answer to #6.
One member dominating	*Everyone is participating equally. Great group!*	*Helen, you are the first to answer every time. Could you be the accuracy checker?*
Groups that have finished	*Your work looks good. Now do the next activity.*	You are being very thorough. But time is almost up.
Group working effectively	*Your group is working so well. What behaviors are helping you?*	What is wrong with the way you are working? Make three plans to solve the problem.

General Advice For Intervening

Tips	Traps
Intervene Only When Absolutely Needed	Jump In Frequently To Solve Problem
Intervene At Eye Level	Stand Over Group, Looking Down
Have Whole Group Focus On You	Have Only One Member Focus On You
Label Actions, Not Student	Embarrass, Insult By Labeling Student
Focus On "Here And Now"	Bring In The Past
Have Students Problem Solve	Tell Students What To Do
Have Students Generate Three Plans	Say "OK" To Students Initial Plan

In one third grade class, the teacher noticed when distributing papers that one student was sitting back away from the other three. A moment later the teacher glanced over and only three students were sitting where four were a moment before. As she watched, the three students came marching over to her and complained that Johnny was under the table and wouldn't come out. *"Make him come out!"* they insisted (the teacher's role: police officer, judge, and executioner). The teacher told them that Johnny was a member of their group and asked what they had tried to solve their problem. *"Tried?"* the puzzled reply. *"Yes, have you asked him to come out?"* the teacher suggested. The group marched back and the teacher continued distributing papers to groups. A moment later the teacher glanced over to their table and saw no heads above the table (which is one way to solve the problem). After a few more minutes, four heads came struggling out from under the table and the group (including Johnny) went back to work with great energy. We don't know what happened under that table, but whatever it was, it was effective. What makes this story even more interesting is that the group received a 100 percent on the paper and later, when the teacher was standing by Johnny's desk, she noticed he had the paper clutched in his hand. The group had given Johnny the paper and he was taking it home. He confided to the teacher that this was the first time he could ever remember earning a 100 on anything in school. (If that was your record, you might slip under a few tables yourself.)

Coaching

While you monitor you may wish to coach students who are using the targetted teamwork skills. Your role as a coach is to challenge students to become competent team members, set teamwork goals for the students and the groups to accomplish, give technical advice on how to do the skills, encourage students to try, and demand that students "hussel" while they are working in learning teams.

Encouraging Self-Monitoring

You encourage self-monitoring by having each student assess how often and well he or she (and other group members) performed the targeted skills and actions. Each group member fills out a checklist or questionnaire. The focus of the questions could be what the member did (I, me), what other members did (you, they), or what all members did (we). Self-assessments ("I" statements) are gathered from group members about how often and how well they individually performed the targeted social skills and other expected behaviors. The "you" statements give students an opportunity to give other group members feedback about which actions were seen as helpful or unhelpful. The "we" statements provide an opportunity for group members to reach consensus about which actions helped or hurt the group's work.

Then the group members use the results to help analyze how well they worked together. For each question group members can sum the frequencies and divide by the number of members to derive an average. Or, each group member can publicly share his or her answers in a "whip." The group whips through members' answers, one question at a time, by giving each group member 30 seconds to share his or her answer to each question with no comment allowed from other group members. A third procedure is having each group member name actions he or she performed that helped the group function more effectively, and then name one action the member to his/her right (or left) performed that also helped the group.

Summary

You always monitor your cooperative learning groups to assess students' academic progress and appropirate use of interpersonal and small group skills. To do so, you must prepare for observing, observe, intervene when it is necessary, and have students assess the quality of their teamwork. You have to decide who will observe (you always do), the sampling plan for roving observers, the observation forms to use (whether structured or unstructured), when and how to intervene, and the forms to use for student self-monitoring. You then have students summarize all the feedback they obtain on their group's functioning to be used in the group processing time at the end of the lesson.

My Checklist for Cooperative Groups

NAME _____ DATE _____

1. When I knew an answer or had an idea, I shared it with the group.

    _____ *all of the time*   _____ *some of the time*

    _____ *most of the time*   _____ *never*

2. When my answer did not agree with someone else's, I tried to find out why.

    _____ *all of the time*   _____ *some of the time*

    _____ *most of the time*   _____ *never*

3. When I did not understand something, I asked questions.

    _____ *all of the time*   _____ *some of the time*

    _____ *most of the time*   _____ *never*

4. When someone else did not understand a problem, I helped him understand.

    _____ *all of the time*   _____ *some of the time*

    _____ *most of the time*   _____ *never*

5. I tried to make the people in the group feel respected.

    _____ *all of the time*   _____ *some of the time*

    _____ *most of the time*   _____ *never*

6. Before I signed my name to the paper, I made sure that I understood all of the question and answers, agreed with them, and was confident that all other members understood the answers.

    _____ *all of the time*   _____ *some of the time*

    _____ *most of the time*   _____ *never*

☯ STUDENT CHECKLIST: Cooperation ☯

I contributed my ideas and information.

|————————————————————————|————————————————————————|
Always   *Sometimes*   *Never*

I asked others for their ideas and information.

|————————————————————————|————————————————————————|
Always   *Sometimes*   *Never*

I summarized all our ideas and information.

|————————————————————————|————————————————————————|
Always   *Sometimes*   *Never*

I asked for help when I needed it.

|————————————————————————|————————————————————————|
Always   *Sometimes*   *Never*

I helped the other members of my group learn.

|————————————————————————|————————————————————————|
Always   *Sometimes*   *Never*

I made sure everyone in my group understood how to do
the school work we were studying.

|————————————————————————|————————————————————————|
Always   *Sometimes*   *Never*

I helped keep the group studying.

|————————————————————————|————————————————————————|
Always   *Sometimes*   *Never*

I included everyone in our work.

|————————————————————————|————————————————————————|
Always   *Sometimes*   *Never*

Chapter Twelve: Providing Closure to the Lesson

Retention of what is learned is much higher when students systematically review what they have learned immediately following a lesson. At the end of the lesson, students should work in small groups (pairs or triads) to reconstruct conceptually what the lesson covered and what they were responsible for learning. Students should recall and summarize the major points in the lesson, organize the material into a conceptual framework, integrate into existing conceptual frameworks, understand where they will use it in future lessons, and identify final questions for the teacher.

The most important issue in providing closure to a lesson is who is does it--the teacher or the students. What you know is that (a) only students can provide closure (it is something that happens internally, not externally), (b) closure is an active, not a passive process, and (c) closure is best created by directly explaining what one has learned to others (to do so a student must formulate, conceptually organize, and summarize what one has learned and is able to monitor and modify the resulting conceptual structure while saying it outloud to a groupmate). Teachers only structure and facilitate student closure, they cannot personally provide it to a student. **Closure is something that comes out, not something that is poured in.** The most effective ways for providing closure are cooperative:

1. Focused discussion groups.

2. Writing pairs.

3. Note-taking pairs.

Closure Cooperative Focused Discussion

Closure is created by students formulating what they know and explaining it to others. Small focused discussion groups are ideal for providing closure. What you, the teacher, do to create closure to the lesson is:

1. Have students meet in their cooperative groups (or assign them to new groups of two or three members).

2. Provide closure to the lesson by giving students the **task** of summarizing what was covered in the lesson and what they learned. The **cooperative goal** is to create one set of answers from the group, members have to agree, and all members have to be able to explain the group's answers. Ask the groups to write down:

   a. What is covered in the lesson.

   b. What are the five most important things you learned?

   c. What are two questions you wish to ask?

   Through the discussion students will conceptually organize what they learned and integrate it into existing conceptual frameworks. The discussion will also point students toward the homework and the next class session.

3. You collect the groups' answers and record them to support the importance of the procedure and see what students have learned. Handing the papers back periodically with brief comments helps reinforce this procedure for students.

Closure Cooperative Writing Pairs

At the end of the lesson, organize students into pairs and give them the **task** of writing a "*one-minute paper*" describing:

1. The major points learned today.

2. The main unanswered questions they still have.

Structure the task coopertively by asking for one paper from each pair of students. Both pair members must agree on what is written, and both must be able to explain it. The joint writing task helps students focus on the central themes of the course. In writing their papers students should write:

1. An introductory paragraph outlining the content of the lesson.

2. Clear conceptual definitions of the concepts and terms presented.

3. A summary of and judgment about the material covered.

4. A description of and judgment about the practical significance of the material covered.

5. Anything the students know beyond what was covered in the lesson.

Closure Cooperative Note-Taking Pairs

Closure note-taking pairs are similar to the cooperative note-taking pairs used inter-mittently during the lesson. Students review and complete their notes, reflecting on the lesson, and writing the major concepts and pertinent information presented. More specifically you:

1. Organize students into pairs.

2. Give them the **task** of writing out complete notes summarizing what was covered in the lesson. The **cooperative goal** is for both students to ensure that they have a complete, comprehensive, and accurate set of notes summarizing what was covered in the lesson.

3. One student summarizes his or her notes to the other. The summary should include:

   a. Here is what I have in my notes.

   b. Here are the key points covered in the lesson.

   c. This is the most surprising thing the teacher said or was stated in the materials today.

4. The other student does the same thing.

5. The two students modify their notes by adding:

   a. What the other student had that they did not.

   b. New insights and information discovered in the discussion.

6. The two students sign each other's notes to indicate that they believe their partner's notes are complete, comprehension, and accurate.

Skill Teaching Planning Form

Cooperative Skill : _____

Definition: _____

_____

Looks Like	Sounds Like

Show need by: _____

_____

_____

Reinforce use while they work by: _____

_____

_____

Refine skill later by: _____

_____

_____

Process use by: _____

_____

_____

Notes on levels of use, problems, things learned for next time:

Section Five: Evaluating And Processing

Adventurous  **A**ssess Student Learning

Explorers **E**valuate

Pursue  **P**rocess Group Effectiveness

Peaks of **P**lan for Improvement

Cooperation **C**elebrate Efforts To Learn

Chapter Thirteen: Evaluating the Quality and Quantity of Learning

Assessing Student Learning

Aesop tells of two travelers who were walking along the seashore. Far out they saw something riding on the waves. *"Look,"* said one, *"a great ship rides in from distant lands, bearing rich treasures!"* As the object came closer, the other said, *"That is not a great treasure ship. It is a fisherman's skiff, with the day's catch of savory fish!"* Still nearer came the object and the waves washed it up on shore. *"It's a chest of gold lost from some wreck,"* they cried. Both travelers rushed to the beach, but there they found nothing but a water-soaked log. The moral of the story is, **Before you reach a conclusion, do a careful assessment**.

Assessment and evaluation of academic learning is part of your responsibility as a teacher. Assessment and evaluation are so intertwined that it is hard to separate them. But generally, **assessment** is collecting data to make a judgment while **evaluation** is judging something's value based on the available data. You can have assessment without evaluation, but you cannot have evaluation without assessment. There are five rules for assessing and evaluating.

Rule One: Conduct all assessment and evaluation in the context of learning teams. You must assess and evaluate each student's achievement, but the assessment is far more effective when it takes place in a team context.

Rule Two: Assess, assess, assess, and assess! The learning groups and their members need continual feedback on the level of learning of each member. You should give frequent tests and quizzes and require lots of written papers and oral presentations.

Evaluating Students' Learning

Rules For Assessing

Assessment Plan

Using Cooperative Procedures:

☐ Prior To Lesson

☐ During Lesson

☐ Following Lesson

Myths About Team-Based Assessment

Assessment Plan

Rule Three: Directly involve students in assessing each other's level of learning. Group members then provide immediate remediation to maximize all group members' learning.

Rule Four: Use a criterion-referenced system for all assessment and evaluation. You should avoid all comparisons among students' level of achievement. Such comparison is a "force for destruction" that will decrease student motivation and learning.

Rule Five: Use a wide variety of assessment formats. Cooperative learning, furthermore, provides an arena in which **total quality learning** (continuous improvement of the process of students helping teammates learn), **performance-based assessment** (requiring students to demonstrate what they can do with what they know by performing a procedure or skill), and **authentic assessment** (requiring students to demonstrate the desired procedure or skill in a "real life" context) can take place.

As a teacher, you make an assessment plan for each of your classes. The assessment plan may focus on:

1. **The Processes Of Learning:** To improve continuously the quality of students' efforts to learn, you must engineer a system whereby the processes students use to learn are assessed. Following the advice of W. Edwards Deming and other advocates of **total quality management,** you focus on assessing and improving processes of learning rather than on assessing outcomes (known as inspecting quality in). In the classroom, this is known as **total quality learning.** The assumption is that if you continuously improve the processes of learning, the quality and quantity of student learning will also continuously improve. To implement total quality, you assign students to teams and the team takes charge of the quality of the work of its members. Team members, therefore, must (a) learn how to define and organize work processes, (b) assess the quality of the processes by recording indicators of progress, and (c) place the measures on a quality chart for evaluating effectiveness.

2. **The Outcomes Of Learning:** To assess how much students have actually learned in a class, you measure directly the quality and quantity of their achievement. Achievement is traditionally assessed by paper-and-pencil tests. The new emphasis, however, is on assessing learning outcomes through performance measures. **Performance-based assessment** requires students to demonstrate what they can do with what they know by performing a procedure or skill. In a performance assessment, the student completes or demonstrates the same behavior that the assessor desires to measure. Students may submit for assessment compositions, exhibitions, demonstrations, video projects, science projects, surveys, and actual job performances. To assess students' performances, you need (a) an appropriate

method of sampling the desired performances and (b) a clearly articulated set of criteria to serve as the basis for evaluative judgments.

Making An Assessment Plan

Performance	Process	Outcomes	Setting
Reading			
Writing			
Math Reasoning			
Presenting			
Problem Solving			
Scientific Reasoning			
Shared Leadership			
Trust Building			

3. **The Setting In Which Assessment Takes Place: Authentic assessment** requires students to demonstrate desired skills or procedures in "real-life" contexts. Since it is impossible to place students in many real-life situations, you may wish to have students complete simulated real-life tasks or solve simulated real-life problems. To conduct an authentic assessment in science, for example, you may assign students to research teams working on a cure for cancer who must (a) conduct an experiment, (b) write a lab report summarizing results, (c) write a journal article, and (d) make an oral presentation at a simulated convention. Like performance-based assessment, to conduct an authentic assessment you need procedures for (a) sampling performances and (b) developing criteria for evaluation. You also need the imagination to find real-life situations or create simulations of them.

Cooperative Learning And Assessment Prior To The Lesson

Prior to the lesson, you must decide on the criteria you will use to evaluate student performance and plan how you will collect the information you need to make judgments. You must also define the process of learning through which students are to reach the criteria.

Cooperative Learning And Assessment During The Lesson

During the lesson, you assess student learning by observing and interviewing students. You cannot measure many learning outcomes (such as level of reasoning, mastery

of problem solving procedures, meta-cognitive thinking) by pencil-and-paper homework assignments and tests. You can assess many cognitive outcomes only by observing students *"thinking outloud."* Cooperative learning groups are *"windows into students' minds."* You (a) assign students to small cooperative groups, (b) give them an assignment, (c) assign one member of each group the role of *"checker for understanding,"* and (d) move from group to group gathering observation data about the quality of the explanations and intellectual interchange occurring among group members. You may gather observation data by (a) using formal observation schedules, checklists, or rating scales and (b) noting anecdotal impressions.

You may wish to train your students to be observers. Cooperative learning groups offer a unique opportunity for immediate diagnosis of level of understanding, immediate feedback from peers, and immediate remediation to correct misunderstandings and fill in gaps in students' understanding. Training students to observe each other's cognitive reasoning will facilitate the cycle of immediate diagnosis-feedback-remediation.

You will wish to interview students to determine their level of cognitive reasoning, problem solving, and meta-cognitive thinking. Meet with a group and randomly select one member to explain the answer to a randomly selected question. When that member finishes responding to the question, other group members can add to the answer. Then ask another member a different question. Repeat this procedure until all questions have been answered. If group members cannot give adequate answers, the group has to return to the assignment and practice until they are better prepared. Give some guidance by identifying particular weaknesses and strengths in the member's answers.

Cooperative Procedures For Assessment Following Lesson

There are numerous ways you can use cooperative procedures following a lesson to help in the assessment process. Following the lesson, you assess student learning with paper-and-pencil tests and performance measures such as completed compositions, presentations, and projects. Homework assignments follow. You may measure student performances in authentic settings. On the basis of the information gathered by the assessments, students set improvement goals and celebrate their hard work and success while you give grades. Many of the most important arenas for assessment are highly labor intensive and can only be conducted frequently if students are involved in the assessment process. Given below are several of the more important.

Checking Homework

Whenever you require homework, you can use cooperative learning groups to assess the quality of each member's work and provide immediate remediation and clarification of anything the students do not understand. The **task** for students is to bring their completed homework to class and understand how to do it correctly. The **cooperative goal** is to ensure that all group members have completed their homework and understand how to do it correctly. The procedures are:

1. Students enter the classroom and meet in their cooperative learning groups. The groups should be heterogeneous in terms of achievement level. One member (the **runner**) goes to the teacher's desk, picks up the group's folder, and hands out any materials in the folder to the appropriate members. The runner records how much of the assignment each member completed.

2. You assign two roles each day: **Explainer** (explains step-by-step how to complete the homework) and **accuracy checker** (verifies that the explanation is accurate, encourages, and provides any needed coaching). The groups rotate the roles clockwise around the group so that each member does an equal amount of explaining.

3. Group members discuss the assignment. They go through the answers to the homework one-by-one to ensure that members agree on the answer and understand the information or procedures required to complete the assignment. If there is disagreement, group members discuss the question until they reach consensus and they all understand how to answer the question correctly. The group should concentrate on the parts of the assignment members do not understand. For any aspect of the homework on which group members do not agree, they have to find the page number and paragraph in the textbook explaining how to complete that part of the assignment.

4. The teacher moves from group to group listening to the explanations and answering students' questions about the homework. The teacher should randomly ask individual students to explain how to complete their homework to ensure that there is a high degree of individual accountability.

5. At the end of the review time, group members place their homework in the group's folder and the runner places it on the teacher's desk. Members can assign each other further homework to ensure that all group members understand the material and procedures being studied.

Giving Tests

You should frequently give tests and quizzes to assess how much each student is learning. Whenever you give a test, cooperative learning groups can serve as bookends by preparing members to take the test and providing a setting in which students review the test. Two of the purposes of testing are to evaluate how much each student knows and assess what students still need to learn. Using the following procedure will result in achieving both purposes. Plus, it will also provide students with immediate clarification of what they did not understand and remediation of what they did not learn. Finally, it prevents arguments between you and your students over which answers are correct and why. The procedure is:

Group
Individual
Group

1. Students prepare for, and review for, a test in cooperative learning groups.

2. Each student takes the test individually, making two copies of his or her answers. Students submit one set of answers to you to grade and keep one set for the group discussion.

3. Students retake the test in their cooperative learning groups.

Preparing For A Test In Cooperative Groups

Students meet in their cooperative groups. You give students (a) study questions and (b) class time to prepare for the examination. The tasks are for students to discuss each study question and come to consensus about its answer. The cooperative goal is to ensure that all group members understand how to answer the question correctly. For any aspect of the assignment for which there is disagreement among group members, students must find the page number and paragraph explaining the relevant procedures or information. When the time is up, the students give each other encouragement for doing well on the upcoming test.

Taking The Test Individually

Each student takes the test individually, making two copies of his or her answers. The task (and individual goal) is to answer each test question correctly. Students submit one copy of the answers to you (the teacher). You score the answers and evaluate student performance against a present criterion of excellence. Students keep one copy for the group discussion. After all group members have finished the test, the group meets to take the test again.

Retaking The Test In Cooperative Groups

Students meet in their cooperative learning groups to retake the test. The **task** is to answer each question correctly. The **cooperative goal** is to ensure that all group members understand the material and procedures covered by the test. Members do so by (a) reaching consensus on the answer for each question and the rationale or procedure underlying the answer and (b) ensuring that all members can explain the answer and the rationale or procedure. The procedure is for members to:

1. Compare their answers on the first question.

2. If there is agreement, one member explains the rationale or procedure underlying the question and the group moves on to question two.

3. If there is disagreement, members find the page number and paragraph explaining the relevant information or procedures. The group is responsible for ensuring that all members understand the material they missed on the test. If necessary, group members assign review homework to each other. When all members agree on the answer and believe other members comprehend the material, the group moves on to question two.

4. The learning groups repeat this procedure until they have covered all test questions.

5. The group members celebrate how hard members have worked in learning the material and how successful they were on the test.

Oral Presentations

Assessment of a student's achievement may be conducted during an oral presentation of what the student has learned. When you require students to give oral presentations, cooperative learning groups can serve as bookends by preparing members to give the presentation and providing a setting in which students review the effectiveness of each member's presentation.

Group
Individual
Group

1. Students prepare their presentations in cooperative learning groups.

2. Each students makes his or her presentation.

3. Students review the effectiveness of their presentations in cooperative learning groups.

Preparing For The Presentation

You assign students to cooperative learning groups of four. You give students a topic to make a presentation on (or let them choose a topic). The learning **tasks** are for students to (a) prepare a presentation, (b) make a presentation to the class, and (c) assess the effectiveness of their presentation. The presentation has to include visuals and/or active participation by the audience. The **cooperative goal** is to ensure that all group members learn the material they study and develop and deliver a high-quality presentation.

You give students the time and resources (such as access to the library or reference materials) to prepare their presentations. Students should make their presentation to their cooperative group and receive critical feedback at least once before they make the presentation to the entire class.

Making The Presentation

You divide the class into four groups and place them in separate corners of the classroom. Each group member simultaneously makes his or her presentation to one-fourth of the class. In this way, all group members make their presentations, demonstrate their mastery of their topic, and are individually accountable for learning the material studied. While students listen to classmates' presentations, they are responsible for determining whether each presentation was:

1. Scholarly and informative.

2. Interesting, concise, easy to follow.

3. Involving (audience active, not passive).

4. Intriguing (audience interesting in finding out more on their own).

Students (a) complete two copies of an assessment form for each presentation, (b) give one copy to the presenter (who takes them back to his or her cooperative group), and (c) give one copy to you (the teacher). You, the teacher, listen to part of each presentation and make your evaluation of its quality.

Assessing The Effectiveness Of The Presentations

Students meet in their cooperative learning groups. Each member shares his or her assessment sheets. The group makes a set of recommendations on how each member may improve his or her presentation skills. The group may assign homework and further practice presenting. Finally, the cooperative learning groups celebrate the hard work and success of their members.

Assessing The Quality Of Oral Presentations

Criterion	Rating	Comments
Scholarly, Informative		
Interesting, Concise, Easy To Follow		
Involving		
Intriguing		
Other:		
Other:		

For each criterion, rate the presentation between 1 (very poor) and 10 (very good).

Portfolios

The peer editing procedure used to assess the quality of writing (see Chapter 11) and oral presentations can also be used to assess the quality of students' portfolios.

Myths About Team-Based Assessment and Evaluation

Myth One: If You Assess Student Learning, You Have To Give The Students Grades. Assessment is collecting data while giving grades is placing your judgment on the student's performance. Although you can use assessment data to determine grades, grading is not the purpose of assessment. Improvement is. Assessment should occur continuously with the data being placed in forms that are understandable to students so that students can make judgments about how to improve.

Myth Two: Teachers Must Read Every Student Paper And Provide Feedback. This is a very destructive myth. Teachers have to require more work than they can possibly judge. Students need ongoing feedback for continuous improvement of learning. The teacher alone cannot provide the amount of feedback students need on a daily basis. With guidance and practice, students can develop the capacity to provide one another with the kind of feedback useful for improvement. This means that students must learn how to observe and collect assessment data. As student involvement in assessment increases, however, teacher involvement does not decrease. The teacher is still responsible for carefully monitoring teamwork and intervening when appropriate to provide immediate feedback. The teacher also provides feedback by sampling student products.

Myth Three: Students Are Not Capable Of Meaningful Involvement In Assessment. Students are capable of assessing their own learning and the learning of their groupmates. They do have to be taught how. Assessment skills are learned like any skill. Students must understand why they are being asked to participate in assessment. They must understand the procedures for doing so. They must gain considerable experience in assessing learning. They must process how well they did. With repeated practice, students will become quite skillful in assessing their own and their groupmates' learning.

Myth Four: Involving Students In Assessment Takes Valuable Time Away From Learning And Lowers Their Achievement. Involving students in assessment has a number of important effects on learning that cannot be achieved any other way. Assessing the quality of groupmates' work (a) enhances the formation of conceptual frameworks, (b) builds a frame of reference to assess the quality of their own work, (c) promotes higher-level reasoning, and (d) increases commitment to promote groupmates' learning. Self and other assessment are essential components of the learning process. Far from wasting students' time, involving students in assessment is a necessary and important part of teaching.

Myth Five: Assessment Is A Teacher Responsibility, Not To Be Done By Students. The teacher is the instructional leader in the classroom and is responsible for creating conditions that make optimal learning possible. Involving students in assessment optimizes their learning and does not change the teacher's responsibility as an instructional leader. Students gain direct and continuous access to data that enable ongoing improvement. Involving students in assessment also increases their commitment to implementing improvements in learning processes.

Myth Six: Individual assessment is lost in team-based approaches to assessment. Team-based approaches to assessment do not eliminate the need for individual assessment. Successful teamwork comes from integrating the proficiencies of every group member to accomplish tasks that each cannot accomplish alone. Assessing individual efforts enables teammates to help, assist, and support one another in the process of improvement.

Summary

After the lesson is over, you must assess the quality and quantity of student learning. Your assessment plan should take into account evaluating the processes students use to learn, the outcomes of their efforts to learn, and the setting in which the learning takes place and is displayed. Assess in the context of learning teams. Assess and evaluate student achievement frequently. Students will gain a great deal by being involved in the assessment process. Make sure you use a criteria referenced evaluation system. In order to assess fairly, use a wide variety of assessment formats. During a lesson you assess by observing the cooperative learning groups and systematically interviewing group members.

Where Does The Teacher's Role Apply?

A	PI	IA	SS	MIP

Step 1: Specifying Objectives
1. Academic
2. Social Skills

Step 2: Making Preinstructional Decisions
1. Decide On Group Size.
2. Assign Students To Groups.
3. Arrange The Room.
4. Arrange Materials.
5. Decide On Roles.
6. Plan Monitoring Procedures And Forms.

Step 3: Setting The Lesson
1. Explain Academic Task And Procedure.
2. Explain Criteria For Success.
3. Structure Cooperation.
4. Structure Individual Accountability.
5. Specify (And Teach) Expected Social Skills.
6. Structure Intergroup Cooperation.

Step 4: Monitoring And Intervening
1. Arrange Face-To-Face Interaction Among Students.
2. Monitor Students' Behavior.
3. Provide Task Assistance.
4. Provide Social Skills Prompting And Encouragement.

Step 5: Evaluating And Processing
1. Evaluate And Celebrate Student Learning.
2. Process Group Functioning And Use Of Social Skills.
3. Provide Closure.

A = Academic, PI = Positive Interdependence, IA = Individual Accountability, SS = Social Skills, MIP = Monitor, Intervene, Process.

Put a check mark in the column(s) to which each aspect of the Teacher's Role applies.

Chapter Fourteen: Group Processing

Aesop tells of the consequences of not processing the effectiveness with which group members work together. A lion had been watching three bulls feeding in an open field. He had tried to attack them several times, but they had kept together, and helped each other to drive him away. The lion had little hope of eating them, for he was no match for three strong bulls with their sharp horns and hoofs. He could not keep away from that field, however, for he could not resist watching a good meal, even when there was little chance of his getting it. One day, however, the bulls had a quarrel. When the hungry lion came to look at them and lick his chops (as he was accustomed to doing), he found them in separate corners of the field. They were as far away from one another as they could get. It was then easy for the lion to attack them one at a time. He did so with the greatest satisfaction and relish. In failing to process their problems in working together and continually increase the effectiveness of their cooperation, the bulls forgot that their success came from their unity.

Processing Starters

1. Name three things your group did well in working together. Name one thing your group could do even better.

2. Think of something each of your group members did that helped the group be effective. Tell them what it is.

3. Tell your group members how much you appreciated their help today.

4. Rate yourself from 1 (low) to 10 (high) on _____ (name a cooperative skill like encouraging participation or checking for understanding). Share your rating with your group and explain why you rated yourself the way you did. Plan how to increase the frequency with which group members use this skill.

Reflecting On And Analyzing Group Effectiveness

At the end of the lesson, students should engage in **group processing**. They reflect on and analyze the group session to (a) describe what member actions were helpful and unhelpful in contributing to the joint efforts to achieve the group's goals and (b) make decisions about what actions to continue or change. The purpose of group processing is to improve continuously the quality of the group's taskwork and teamwork. It also increases individual accountability through focusing attention on each members' responsible and skillful actions to learn and to help groupmates learn. A common teaching error is to provide too brief a time for students to process the quality of their teamwork. Group processing occurs at two levels; there is both small group processing and whole-class processing. There are four parts to group processing.

1. **Feedback:** You ensure that each student and each group and the class receives (and gives) feedback on the effectiveness of taskwork and teamwork.

2. **Reflection:** You ensure that students analyze and reflect on the feedback they receive.

3. **Improvement Goals:** You help individuals and groups set goals for improving the quality of their work.

4. **Celebration:** You encourage the celebration of members' hard work and the group's success.

Giving Personal Feedback In A Helpful, Non Threatening Way

1. **Focus feedback on behavior** (not on personality traits).

2. **Be descriptive** (not judgmental).

3. **Be specific and concrete** (not general or abstract).

4. **Make feedback immediate** (not delayed).

5. **Focus on positive actions** (not negative ones).

6. **Present feedback in a visual** (such as a graph or chart) as well as auditory fashion (not just spoken words alone).

Giving And Receiving Feedback

You take the first step in structuring group processing when you ensure that learning groups and individual students receive feedback on the quality of their taskwork and teamwork so they can continuously improve both. Feedback is information on actual performance that individuals compare with criteria for ideal performance. **When feedback is given skillfully, it generates energy, directs the energy toward constructive action, and transforms the energy into action towards improving the performance of the teamwork skills.** Student performance improves and the discrepancy between actual and real performance decreases. Increased self-efficacy tends to result. Students tend to feel empowered to be even more effective next time. The following **checklist** may help in assessing the effectiveness of feedback.

Feedback Checklist

Feedback	Yes	No, Start Over
Is Feedback Given?		Was Not Given Or Received, Start Over
Is Feedback Generating Energy In Students?		Students Are Indifferent, Start Over
Is Energy Directed Towards Identifying And Solving Problems So Performance Is Improved?		Energy Used To Resist, Deny, Avoid Feedback, Start Over
Do Students Have Opportunities To Take Action To Improve Performance?		No, Students Are Frustrated, Feel Like Failures, Start Over

Processing Quickies

Our group is really good at…

The best thing that happened today was…

Some words to describe our group are…

Today our group discovered…

Today I really helped my group by…

Today I learned…

We are a super-team because…

Next time we will be better at…

Group Processing

Receive Feedback

Analyze And Reflect

Set Improvement Goals

Celebrate

Ensuring Every Group Member Receives Positive Feedback

1. Having each group focus on one member at a time. Members tell the target person one thing he/she did that helped them learn or work together effectively. The focus is rotated until all members have received positive feedback.

2. Having members write a positive comment about each other member's participation on an index card. The students then give their written comments to each other so thatevery member will have, in writing, positive feedback from all the other group members.

3. Having members comment on how well each other member used the social skills by writing an answer to one of the following statements. The students then give their written statements to each other.

   a. I appreciated it when you...

   b. I liked it when you...

   c. I admired you when you...

   d. I enjoyed it when you...

   e. You really helped out the group when you...

This procedure may also be done orally. In this case students look at the member they are complimenting, use his or her name, and give their comments. The person receiving the positive feedback makes eye contact and says nothing or "thank you." Positive feedback should be directly and clearly expressed and should not be brushed off or denied.

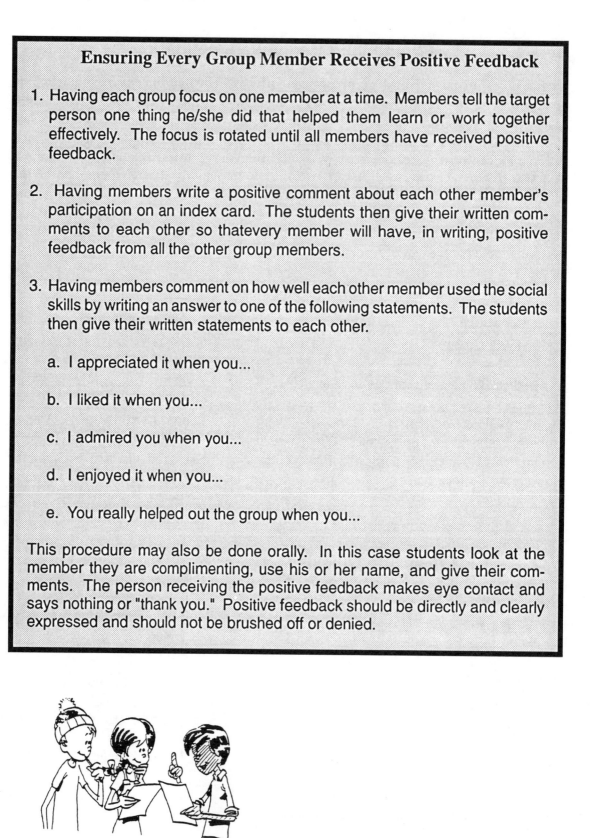

Analyzing Data On Group Effectiveness

You take the second step in structuring group processing when you have students reflect on and analyze the group session they just completed to discover what helped and what hindered the quality of learning and whether specific behaviors had a positive or negative effect. Varying the procedures for analyzing and reflecting on the data collected about members interactions keeps group processing vital and interesting. Ways of doing so include having each group:

1. Plot in a chart the data on members' interaction. Two of the most helpful charting procedures are the Bar Chart and the Run Chart.

2. Do a mind-map representing the secrets of the group's success.

3. Rate themselves on a series of dimensions on a bar chart.

4. Give each member 60 seconds to identify three things other members did to help groupmates learn.

5. Discuss the effective use of teamwork skills by members (*"How did other group members encourage participation?" "How did other group members check for understanding?"*). Each group member gives his or her response and then consensus is achieved through discussion.

A good way for teachers to stay in touch with the functioning of each learning group is to have each group summarize its processing and place its summary in a folder with its completed academic work. The folder is handed in to the teacher each class session. Making the last question on an assignment sheet a group-processing question, furthermore, signals to students that group processing is an integral part of learning.

Long-Term Progress: Weekly Bar Chart

Group Members: _____

_____

Class: _____ Subject Area: _____

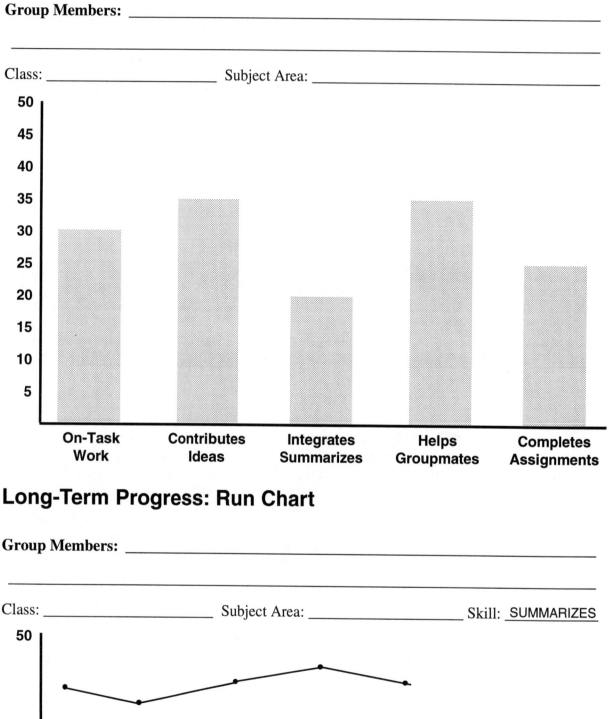

Long-Term Progress: Run Chart

Group Members: _____

_____

Class: _____ Subject Area: _____ Skill: SUMMARIZES

Long-Term Group Progress: Weekly Report Form

Group Members: _____

_____

Class: _____ Subject Area: _____

Date	On-Task Work	Contributes Ideas	Integrates Summarizes	Helps Groupmates	Completes Assignments
Totals:					

Comments: _____

_____

_____

Whole Class Processing

In addition to small group processing, teachers should periodically conduct whole-class processing sessions.

1. **You can share your observations with the whole class.** Charting the data to get a continuous record of class improvement is always a good idea. You make a large chart on which you record the frequency with which students' performed each targeted skill. Students can see how much they improved over time. You may wish to give the class a reward when the class total exceeds a preset criterion of excellence. Not only does such a chart visually remind students of the skills they should practice while working in their groups, but continuous improvement becomes a challenge that promotes class cooperation.

2. **You can add together the observation results of the student observers for an overall class total.** You may wish to chart this data.

3. **You can ask students to** (a) describe things they did to help each other learn, (b) discuss members' answers in the group for a minute or two and arrive at a consensus on an answer, (c) share their group's answer with the class as a whole. Since this procedure takes some time, three questions may be as many as you will wish to ask.

Students do not learn from experiences that they do not reflect on. If the learning groups are to function better tomorrow than they did today, members must receive feedback, reflect on how their actions may be more effective, and plan how to be even more skillful during the next group session.

Group Processing

Write Down Two Ways Each Member Helped The Group Today!

Name	Helpful Action	Helpful Action
•		
•		
•		

Group Processing

Agree On Your Answers And Write On Your Group Paper:

1. **What are three specific actions we did that helped us do well on the assignment?**
   a.
   b.
   c.

2. **How did each of us contribute to the group's success?**
   a.
   b.
   c.

3. **What is an action that would help us do even better next time?**
   a.
   b.
   c.

Set Improvement Goals

You take the third step in structuring group processing when you encourage students to set improvement goals. After analyzing the observational and self-assessment data, reflecting on its meaning, and giving each other feedback, **group members set improvement goals specifying how they will act more skillfully in the next group session**. Students should publicly announce the behavior they plan to increase. They should write the goal down and review it at the beginning of the next group session. **Goal setting is the link between how students did today and how well they will do tomorrow.** Goal setting can have powerful impact on students' behavior as there is a sense of ownership of and commitment to actions that a student has decided to engage in (as opposed to assigned behaviors). **Some procedures for goal setting are:**

1. Have students set specific behavioral goals for the next group session. Have each student pick a specific social skill to use more effectively (an "I" focus) and/or have the group reach consensus about which collaborative skill all group members will practice in the next session (a "we" focus). You can ask the group to hand in a written statement specifying which social skill each member is going to emphasize during the next work session.

2. In a whole-class processing session, ask each group to agree on one conclusion to the statement, "*Our group could do better on social skills by...,*" and tell their answer to the entire class. You write the answers on the board under the title "goals." At the beginning of the next cooperative learning lesson, you publicly read over the goal statements and remind students what they agreed to work on during this session.

3. Have each student write an answer to one of the following questions before the next cooperative learning session:

   a. "*Something I plan to do differently next time to help my group is...*"

   b. "*The social skill I want to use next time is...*"

   c. "*How I can help my group next time is...*"

   d. "*The things I will do to help my group next time are...*"

   e. "*One social skill I will practice more consistently next time is...*"

4. As an optional activity, have students plan where (outside class) they can apply the social skills they are learning in class. Ask them to make connections between the cooperative learning groups and the rest of their lives. Have them specify times in the hallway, playground, home, church, or community where they can use the same social skills they are learning in class. Both "I" and "we" focuses are useful.

Date _____

We Will _____
                    (Behavior)
_____ Times Today
        (Number)

Signed _____   _____

_____   _____

Date _____

Next Time We Will Be

Better At _____
                    (Behavior)

Signed: _____   _____

_____   _____

Celebrating

You take the fourth step in structuring group processing when you have group members celebrate their success and members' efforts to learn. Group processing ends with students celebrating their hard work and the success of their cooperative learning group. Celebrations are key to encouraging students to persist in their efforts to learn (Johnson & Johnson, 1993). Long-term, hard, persistent efforts to learn come more from the heart than from the head. Being recognized for efforts to learn and to contribute to groupmates' learning reaches the heart more effectively than do grades or tangible rewards. Both small-group and whole-class celebrations should take place. Small group processing provides the means to celebrate the success of the group and reinforce the positive behaviors of group members. Individual efforts that contribute to the group's success are recognized and encouraged. Members' actions aimed at helping groupmates learn are perceived, respected, and recognized. It is feeling successful, appreciated, and respected that builds commitment to learning, enthusiasm about working in cooperative groups, and a sense of self-efficacy about subject-matter mastery and working cooperatively with classmates.

A common teaching error is to provide too brief a time for students to process the quality of their cooperation. Students do not learn from experiences that they do not reflect on. If the learning groups are to function better tomorrow than they did today, students must receive feedback, reflect on how their actions may be more effective, and plan how to be even more skillful during the next group session.

Obstacles To Group Processing

Some of the common obstacles to group processing are given below (Dishon & O'Leary, 1984). For each obstacle a number of solutions are suggested.

1. **There is not enough time for group processing.** For many reasons (fire drills, announcements, assemblies, discipline problems) teachers often believe that they cannot take the time for group processing that day, week, or month. When such an attitude dominates, some suggestions are:

   a. Do quick processing by rapidly asking the class to tell how well their groups are functioning. Make a statement and have students indicate agreement or disagreement by: **agree** (hand in air), **do not know** (arms folded), **disagree** (hands down). You can make two or three statements and get students' responses in a minute or so.

   b. Do processing now and either have students finish the work at home or else do it tomorrow in class.

2. **Processing stays vague.** When students conclude, "*We did OK,*" "*We did a good job,*" or "*Everyone was involved,*" the teacher knows that the processing is not specific enough. Some suggested remedies are:

   a. Use specific statements students have to give detailed responses to.

   b. Use student observers so that specific frequencies of behaviors are recorded.

   c. Give groups specific questions to be answered about their functioning.

3. **Students stay uninvolved in processing.** Occasionally there will be groups where members consistently stay uninvolved in analyzing the group's functioning. In such a case, try:

   a. Asking for a written report from the group reporting the strengths and weaknesses of their functioning.

   b. Using processing sheets that require participation from everyone.

c. Assigning to the student most uninvolved in the processing the job of recorder or spokesperson for the group.

d. Having all members sign the processing statement to indicate they participated in the group processing and agree with the group's conclusions.

e. Giving bonus points for group processing reports.

4. **Written process reports are incomplete or messy.** There may be groups who hand in incomplete or messy reports of their group processing. You may wish to try:

a. Having group members sign each other's processing sheets to show that each has been checked for completeness and neatness.

b. Giving bonus points for neatness and completeness.

5. **Students use poor cooperative skills during processing.** When group members do not listen carefully to each other, when they are afraid to contribute to the processing, when the discussion becomes divisive, the teacher may wish to intervene by:

a. Assigning specific roles for the processing.

b. Having one group member observe the processing and have the group discuss the results.

Summary

Group processing is the key to continuous improvement. Without group processing, ineffective practices will tend to continue and the potential of the learning group will tend not to be realized. There are four steps to ensuring that students engage in effective group processing. Students must receive feedback on the effectiveness of their actions in trying to learn and help groupmates learn. Students must reflect on the feedback. Students then set improvement goals specifying how they will act more skillfully in the next group session. Finally, students celebrate their hard work and the success of their learning group.

A common teaching error is to provide too brief a time for students to process the quality of their teamwork. Some of the keys to successful small group processing are allowing sufficient time for it to take place, providing a structure for processing (such as "*List three things your group is doing well today and one thing you could improve*"), emphasizing positive feedback, making the processing specific rather than general, maintaining student involvement in processing, reminding students to use their cooperative skills while they process, and communicating clear expectations as to the purpose of processing.

Teacher Observation Form

GROUPS	EXPLAINING CONCEPTS	ENCOURAGING PARTICIPATION	CHECKING UNDERSTANDING	ORGANIZING THE WORK
1				
2				
3				
4				
5				

Chapter Fifteen: Summary And Conclusions

Sandy Koufax was one of the greatest pitchers in the history of baseball. Although he was naturally talented, he was also unusually well trained and disciplined. He was perhaps the only major-league pitcher whose fastball could be heard to hum. Opposing batters, instead of talking and joking around in the dugout, would sit quietly and listen for Koufax's fastball to hum. When it was their turn to bat, they were already intimidated. There was, however, a simple way for Koufax's genius to have been negated. By making David (the first author of this book) his catcher. To be great, a pitcher needs an outstanding catcher (his great partner was Johnny Roseboro). David is such an unskilled catcher that Koufax would have had to throw the ball much, much slower in order for David to catch it. This would have deprived Koufax of his greatest weapon. Placing Roger and Edythe at key defensive positions in the infield or outfield, furthermore, would have seriously affected Koufax's success. Sandy Koufax was not a great pitcher on his own. Only as part of a team could Koufax achieve greatness. In baseball and in the classroom it takes a cooperative effort. Extraordinary achievement comes from a cooperative group, not from the individualistic or competitive efforts of an isolated individual.

Like Sandy Koufax, natural talent is not enough to make a great student. Students must be part of a team in order to realize their full potential. While some students may seek out friends to study with outside of school, you increase the power of your teaching through the use of cooperative learning. When students are used to working alone it takes courage to assign them to groups and structure cooperation. Change always requires courage. But remember, "it is only daring educators who make instructional excellence possible." You dare to create the possibility of instructional excellence when you assign students to small groups and require students to work together to maximize their own and each other's learning. The essence of cooperative learning is positive interdependence where students recognize that "*we are all in this together, sink or swim.*" Other basic elements of cooperation include individual accountability (where every student is accountable for both learning the assigned material and helping other group members learn), face-to-face interaction among students within which students promote each other's success, students appropriately using interpersonal and small group skills, and students processing how effectively their learning group is functioning. The research provides exceptionally strong evidence that cooperation results in greater effort to achieve, more positive interpersonal relationships, and greater psychological health than do competitive or individualistic efforts (Johnson & Johnson, 1989).

There are three types of cooperative learning groups--formal cooperative learning groups, informal cooperative learning groups, and cooperative base groups. This book has concentrated primarily on formal and informal cooperative learning. To understand all three types of cooperative learning groups, see Johnson, Johnson, and Holubec (1992, 1993).

In completing this book you have finished completed one journal and are about to begin another (the use of cooperative learning in your classroom). Your journal will be memorable and successful if you remember a number of key things. First, you have to remember, *"Daring educators make instructional excellence possible."* If you can remember that, you can remember the teacher's role in conducting a cooperative lesson:

1. Make pre-instructional decisions.

2. Explain the learning task and cooperative structure.

3. Monitor student learning groups and intervene when necessary.

4. Evaluate academic learning and have groups process their effectiveness.

Once you remember the overall framework of conducting the lesson, you need to remember each part. First, you remember, *"O Scram."* To conduct a cooperative lesson, you must decide on your academic and social skills objectives. You must decide what size of groups to use, how to assign students to groups, and how long the groups will work together. You must decide which roles to assign the group members. You must decide how best to arrange the room. You must plan your instructional materials.

Second, you remember, *"Task Criteria PIE."* You must explain to students what they are to do during the lesson. You give a clear academic assignment and explain the criteria for success. You explain the positive interdependence that binds students together as they work on the lesson and binds groups together as they all work to learn. You explain the ways in which each individual group member will be held accountable for doing his or her fair share of the work. You explain the teamwork skills students are expected to use during the lesson.

Third, you remember, *"MITT."* You conduct the lesson and, while students work together cooperatively, you monitor the learning groups and intervene when it is needed to improve their taskwork and teamwork. You provide closure to the lesson when the time is over.

Fourth, you remember, *"Adventurous explorers pursue peaks of cooperation."* You structure the post-lesson activities. You assess students' academic learning and evaluate the level of students' performance. You structure group processing so that the students reflect on and analyze how effectively they and their learning groups functioned during the lesson. They set improvement goals. Finally, the members of each group celebrate their hard work and success.

You are now ready to start over with *"Daring educators make instructional excellence possible"* for the next lesson.

One of the things we have been told many times by teachers who have mastered the use of cooperative learning is, *"Don't say it is easy!"* We know it's not. It can take years to become an expert. There is a lot of pressure to teach like everyone else, to have students learn alone, and not to let students look at each other's papers. Students will not be accustomed to working together and are likely to have a competitive orientation. You may wish to start small by using cooperative learning for one topic or in one class until you feel comfortable, and then expand into other topics or classes. **Implementing cooperative learning in your classroom takes disciplined effort. It is not easy. But it is worth it.**

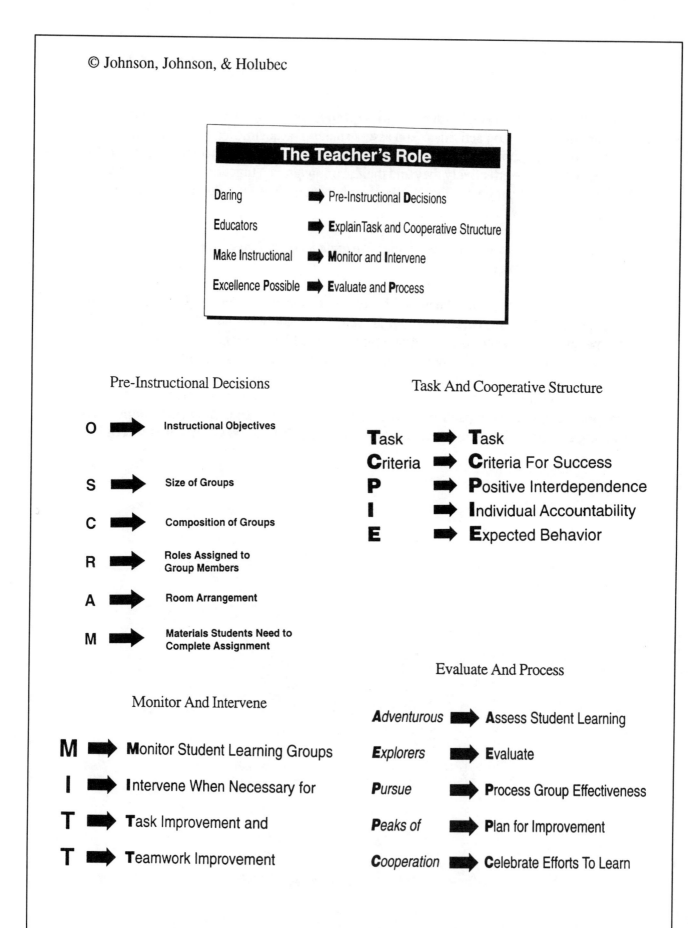

The Teacher's Role

Daring ➡ Pre-Instructional **D**ecisions

Educators ➡ **E**xplainTask and Cooperative Structure

Make Instructional ➡ **M**onitor and **I**ntervene

Excellence Possible ➡ **E**valuate and **P**rocess

Pre-Instructional Decisions

O ➡ **Instructional Objectives**

S ➡ **Size of Groups**

C ➡ **Composition of Groups**

R ➡ **Roles Assigned to Group Members**

A ➡ **Room Arrangement**

M ➡ **Materials Students Need to Complete Assignment**

Task And Cooperative Structure

Task ➡ **T**ask

Criteria ➡ **C**riteria For Success

P ➡ **P**ositive Interdependence

I ➡ **I**ndividual Accountability

E ➡ **E**xpected Behavior

Monitor And Intervene

M ➡ **M**onitor Student Learning Groups

I ➡ **I**ntervene When Necessary for

T ➡ **T**ask Improvement and

T ➡ **T**eamwork Improvement

Evaluate And Process

Adventurous ➡ **A**ssess Student Learning

Explorers ➡ **E**valuate

Pursue ➡ **P**rocess Group Effectiveness

Peaks of ➡ **P**lan for Improvement

Cooperation ➡ **C**elebrate Efforts To Learn

References

Aronson, E. (1978). **The jigsaw classroom.** Beverly Hills, CA: Sage Publications.

Dishon, D., O'Leary, P. (1984). **A guidebook for cooperative learning**. Holmes Beach, FL: Learning Publications.

Deutsch, M. (1949b). A theory of cooperation and competition. **Human Relations, 2**, 129-152.

DeVries, D., & Edwards, K. (1974). Student teams and learning games: Their effects on cross-race and cross-sex interaction. **Journal of Educational Psychology, 66**, 741-749.

Johnson, D. W. (1970). Social psychology of education. New York: Holt, Rinehart, & Winston.

Johnson, D. W. (1979). Educational psychology. Englewood Cliffs, NJ: Prentice-Hall.

Johnson, D. W. (1991). **Human relations and your career** (3rd ed.). Englewood Cliffs, NJ: Prentice-Hall.

Johnson, D. W. (1993). **Reaching out: Interpersonal effectiveness and self-actualization** (6th ed.). Needham Heights, MA: Allyn & Bacon.

Johnson, D. W., & Johnson, F. (1994). **Joining together: Group theory and group skills** (5th ed.). Needham Heights, MA: Allyn & Bacon.

Johnson, D. W., Johnson, R., & Holubec, E. (1983). Circles of learning (Video). Edina, MN: Interaction Book Company.

Johnson, D. W., & Johnson, R. (1989). **Cooperation and competition: Theory and research.** Edina, MN: Interaction Book Company.

Johnson, D. W., & Johnson, R. (1991a). **Teaching students to be peacemakers.** Edina, MN: Interaction Book Company.

Johnson, D. W., & Johnson, R. (1992a). **Creative controversy: Intellectual challenge in the classroom.** Edina, MN: Interaction Book Company.

Johnson, D. W., & Johnson, R. (1993). **Leading the cooperative school** (2nd Edition). Edina, MN: Interaction Book Company.

Johnson, D. W., & Johnson, R. (1975/1994). **Learning together and alone: Cooperative, competitive, and individualistic learning.** Englewood Cliffs, NJ: Prentice-Hall.

Johnson, D. W., Johnson, R., & Holubec, E. (1992). **Advanced cooperative learning.** Edina, MN: Interaction Book Company.

Johnson, D. W., Johnson, R., & Holubec, E. (1993). **Cooperation in the classroom** (6th ed.). Edina, MN: Interaction Book Company.

Johnson, D. W., Johnson, R., & Smith, K. (1991). **Active learning: Cooperative in the college classroom.** Edina, MN: Interaction Book Company.

Johnson, R., & Johnson, D. W. (1985). **Warm-ups, grouping strategies, and group activities**. Edina, MN: Interaction Book Company.

Kagan, S. (1988). **Cooperative learning.** San Juan Capistrano, CA: Resources for Teachers.

Kouzes, J., & Posner, B. (1987). **The leadership challenge**. San Francisco: Jossey-Bass.

Stevenson, H., & Stigler, J. (1992). **The learning gap.** New York: Summit.